Thirsty

Tom Gilbey has spent his whole working life in wine. From his start in winemaking to running a flagship City wine merchant, Tom's unwavering passion for wine is part of his DNA and shines through in every wine his company promotes and every wine event he does. His energetic videos answering wine questions are increasingly popular online, especially since his video tasting twenty-five glasses of wine while running the London Marathon went viral. Tom has more than 800,000 followers across Instagram and TikTok.

THIRSTY

100 Great Wines and Stories

Tom Gilbey, aka the Wine Guy

SQUARE PEG

7 9 10 8

Square Peg, an imprint of Vintage, is part of the
Penguin Random House group of companies

Vintage, Penguin Random House UK, One Embassy Gardens,
8 Viaduct Gardens, London SW11 7BW

penguin.co.uk/vintage
global.penguinrandomhouse.com

First published by Square Peg in 2025

Copyright © Tom Gilbey 2025

The moral right of the author has been asserted

Illustrations © Hugo Guinness

Penguin Random House values and supports copyright. Copyright fuels creativity, encourages diverse voices, promotes freedom of expression and supports a vibrant culture. Thank you for purchasing an authorised edition of this book and for respecting intellectual property laws by not reproducing, scanning or distributing any part of it by any means without permission. You are supporting authors and enabling Penguin Random House to continue to publish books for everyone. No part of this book may be used or reproduced in any manner for the purpose of training artificial intelligence technologies or systems. In accordance with Article 4(3) of the DSM Directive 2019/790, Penguin Random House expressly reserves this work from the text and data mining exception.

Typeset in 12.5/15.2pt Garamond Premier Pro by Six Red Marbles UK, Thetford, Norfolk
Printed and bound in Great Britain by Clays Ltd, Elcograf S.p.A.

The authorised representative in the EEA is Penguin Random House Ireland,
Morrison Chambers, 32 Nassau Street, Dublin D02 YH68

A CIP catalogue record for this book is available from the British Library

ISBN 9781529951479

Penguin Random House is committed to a sustainable future
for our business, our readers and our planet. This book is made
from Forest Stewardship Council® certified paper.

To Caroline Gilbey, my dear mum

Contents

Welcome: Greetings from the Wine Guy   1
Introduction   3

1. First Glass   11
   How Wine is Made   *38*

2. Wine Work   45
   How to Taste Wine   *71*

3. First Love   77
   How to Talk 'Wine' (Without Sounding Naff)   *97*

4. F**k France   105
   How to Read a Wine Label   *123*

5. Business Balls-Ups . . . I've had a few   129
   How to Start and Grow a Wine Collection   *157*

6. Swordfights & Sommeliers   161
   How to Choose Wine in a Restaurant   *181*

7. Good Shit   187
   Ten-Step Cheat-sheet on Natural vs Organic and Biodynamic Wines   *204*

CONTENTS

8. Wine Money 209
   Ten Reasons Why Your Wine Might Smell Like Your Granny's Cardigan 225

9. Glitz & Fizz 231
   The Idiot's Guide to Serving Wine – or How Not to Look Like a Plonker 246

10. Blind Tasting 253
    How to Blind Taste Wine . . . Under Pressure 271

Afterword 277
Glossary 279
Acknowledgements 285

Welcome: Greetings from the Wine Guy

Thank you for picking up this book. A book about me, I'm afraid . . . and quite a lot of wine. But this isn't a 'wine book', at least not in the traditional sense. There are very many such books out there, reference guides far better than I could ever write, many of which I own and cherish.

Thirsty is a bit different. It's a book of stories, revealing the ups and downs of my life in wine – plus a curated list of 100 bottles – and, as you'll find out if you read a bit further, it's also an exploration of why wine is at the very centre of my being, and how it can enrich our lives. Some say wine is a drink for crusty old dads. For me, it's an elixir made and sold by passionate eccentrics who've taught me to adventure as far into the glass as I dare – no inhibitions, no right, no wrong, no price too low or too high . . . and it's been a blast.

And, crucially, it's been a jolly good time getting to know you all and making this Wine Wanker (as my son and business partner Fred has christened me) book for you, reader. Without your support and curiosity for the endless jollies I somehow wind up on, none of this would be possible. So, cheers, and please, charge your glass, ideally with a cool white, pink or orange, or a mellow red, or perhaps something bubbly, and join me, reminiscing on a life filled with wine . . .

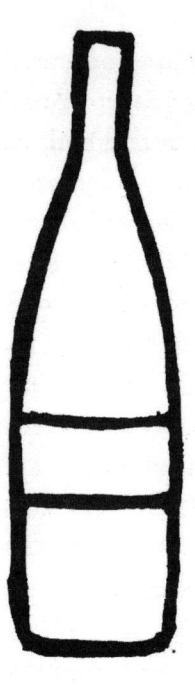

Introduction

Wine has been in my veins, not literally of course, from the moment I popped into this world, over half a century ago. A family affair, my mum and dad made their living from it, running a wine bar and restaurant on Eton High Street, across the bridge from Windsor Castle in Berkshire. (We lived in a little village thirty minutes' drive away, Waltham Saint Lawrence, right in the centre, handily enough next door to the village pub.) But the Gilbeys' love of wine started long before then. Our ancestors have been in the booze trade since the nineteenth century, and in the 1940s, my family was responsible for the sale of a third of all bottles of wine in the UK. Called, imaginatively, Gilbeys and most famous for their gin, the old family firm also came up with one of the most successful Anglo-French wine collaborations of all time, Le Piat d'Or, a label launched in 1978 which, by 1983, was the most popular bottle of red on the UK's shelves.

It all started in 1857 with my great-great-great-grandfather, Alfred Gilbey, and his older brother Walter, who had returned the previous year from the Crimean War without a brass farthing to rub together, nor any particular skills. Either unwilling, or incapable of getting proper jobs, on the advice of their elder brother Henry, himself a partner in a wholesale wine merchants, the young duo started importing good, cheap plonk from the Cape, South Africa, which they flogged from a six-foot trestle table on Oxford Street in London's West End. Victorian bargain-booze-basement, I think you'd best describe it, but their South African wines proved so popular that after three years W. and A. Gilbey boasted over 20,000 happy customers. Ten years on, things were going so swimmingly that they'd progressed from their humble trestle table to owning their own office headquarters at one of the swankiest addresses on Oxford Street, the grand old Pantheon Theatre and Concert Hall – now home to Marks & Spencer.

By 1867 they'd also set up a gin distillery in Camden Town and begun to import wine from France . . . because it was cheaper. Oh yes, those two were quite the Robin Hoods of the wine world – making good grog available to all . . . and pocketing more than a few bob along the way, of course. Indeed, my Gilbey ancestors, for many years, were nailing it in the booze trade and, to top it all, in 1875, they were one of the first English families to buy a French vineyard, the seventeenth-century Château Loudenne, a large Bordeaux estate on the banks of the Gironde, in the Médoc. Well, it's not exactly the *magnifique* Château Lafite Rothschild and definitely not a wine on which I'd stake my own reputation; nevertheless, those redoubtable and most enterprising Victorian brothers had their very own château. Visiting there now, you will find a museum displaying all the old vineyard tools, and sepia photographs of my ancestors with their handlebar moustaches, drinking tea in the garden and smoking pipes in thick tweed suits . . . in June. They were on the map.

Château Loudenne's vineyards roll onto beautifully

INTRODUCTION

manicured gardens which, in turn, roll straight down to the Gironde, the whopping estuary that leads to the Atlantic – and to Britain. The Gilbey brothers shipped thousands of barrels of the château wine home to London, and to their warehouses and bottling plant, sited alongside what is now the Camden Roundhouse arts venue. The Roundhouse itself was the turning depot for the trains which then left the warehouses, packed with Gilbeys booze to distribute throughout the country. Business was booming and before long Gilbeys were distilling their own spirits, Gilbeys Gin and Scotch Whisky.

The Gilbey passion for booze, but wine in particular, passed down through the generations, and such was this heritage that I'm not so sure some didn't end up in my bottle as a toddler. No wonder then that I too followed in the family tradition. I've spent my whole working life in the wine trade, and it has taken me to places in the world I'd never otherwise have seen. And I'm still thirsty. Thirsty for more wine, more celebrations, flavours, travels and experiences. Thirsty for life, in fact, and for me, wine is always at the very heart of it. It's the rich fuel for my enduring curiosity, enquiry and endeavours. I love that I will *never* know everything about wine; I love that it keeps evolving and diversifying; and that it keeps on delivering me new adventures and friendships. And that is the vital heartbeat of this book.

As my clapped-out, health-and-safety-defying bookshelves can attest, hundreds of terrific books have been written about wine. Their authors have taught me how to taste it, where it's grown, how to buy it, but in *Thirsty* my aim is to cover something a bit different. For starters, here you will find no lists of dos and don'ts. In *my* book, there's no right or wrong way to drink or taste wine. If the most expensive red wine from Bordeaux is your bag, slurped from a coffee mug, then that's absolutely fine – well actually, I'm no purist, but at least make sure the coffee cup's clean. That said, I can't tell you how many hours I've spent sitting through 'proper' wine tastings where people discuss malolactic fermentation and soil composition, and, yes, that's all fascinating stuff. But, for me, the real joy of tasting wine is much less complicated than that. It's about discovery. About finding something new in something as old as wine. Every bottle is a potential adventure, every glass a chance to taste something I've never tasted before. Yes, sometimes that quest serves me a corked wine or one that tastes like it's been filtered through an old man's sock. That's all part of the fun, though. Because when I find a good one – a *really* good one – it's pure joy in a glass. And I'm certainly not going to spit it out.

I want to show you *how* and *why* to love a wine – regardless of how expensive it is, what country it comes from, what colour it is, and even whether you think it's any good or not. Believe me, just like you, I've tasted some ropey stuff in my time. Sometimes it's while a 'wine expert' is extolling the virtues of said filth, too, preaching to me that it is 'a quite magnificent vintage', and that it's this, that and everything else. Well, it's for *me* to decide whether it's magnificent or not, as it is for you as you thumb through this book, glass in hand, I hope.

I've never been one for being over-pedantic or getting too serious about the whole shebang. Wine transcends generations and is a drink best shared, over a meal with friends old and new, family and laughter. When the bottle begins to be the focus of the meal or the conversation, that's when, I think,

INTRODUCTION

it begins to lose its magic. When I pour a glass for anybody, the most I want to hear is, 'Holy sh*t, Tom, what's that? It's the nuts.' Then we can crack on with the fun stuff. And it's fine, too, to offer no reaction at all – just simple contentment as the wine oils the wheels of happiness.

For me, the fun in my life has been in growing to really love and appreciate wine and everything that goes with it, before it and around it – I love the food, the places, the people, the history and the culture. I also love the fact that wine is *not* just to be enjoyed by some elite few – it's accessible for all of us. Hell, the Romans chugged it down like water, and I've seen many a French wine grower dispensing their wine to their friends via petrol pumps, straight from the barrels; and now, even here in the UK, the humblest village or corner shop will probably stock something drinkable, maybe even good. Yet somehow it also inspires poets and politicians – lyrical wine enthusiasts may be too many to single out, but Churchill is reputed to have drunk a bottle of Pol Roger Champagne every day of his (adult, I hope) life.

I've peppered this book with stories from my past – those that I can remember – and a bit of history, too. I talk about a few characters who've had a big influence on my life, and many more I've crossed paths with. Wine brings people together. As I type, I recall pouring a glass of Sancerre for Stirling Moss, the British motor racing legend, one Saturday morning in 1991, aged nineteen, at my family's restaurant, the Eton Wine Bar. It was just him sitting on one side of the bar, me behind, and no one else in the restaurant. As Mr Moss chomped his way through a smoked mackerel pâté and sipped from his glass, we got chatting about wine (safer territory to me than Formula One racing) and he insisted I join him for a glass of Sancerre so I too, he told me, could smell the fresh hedgerow, cut grass and gooseberries.

Thirsty is about how I got into wine, how I learned about it. It's about how sometimes I've ballsed things up with wine and how I've gained confidence with every new adventure. It's the journey from my Francophile beginnings to my realisation that there is life beyond Beaujolais. It takes me from revelations in Australia to wines discovered in Bulgaria and beyond, and at the end of each chapter I've added a few takeaways that have been the building blocks of my learning, and a list of ten wines that have made me gaze at the ceiling in wonder – not necessarily the most expensive wines I've ever tried, but the ones that have really stood out for me.

At the start of each chapter I've put my 'hero bottle'. Each of these bottles has been the inspiration for its chapter – not necessarily a masterpiece but a marker in time for me. One that will always bring a smile to my face.

Making mistakes has been integral to my growing to love wine. Disappointments in restaurants, wild choices in wine shops, and leaving bottles to age too long – the litany continues. Crucial, too, has been tasting, both taking part in organised tastings with the wine growers and the trade, and sharing bottles and glasses with friends, rejoicing in the successes and remembering those occasional disappointments.

I suppose my point is that I didn't learn to love wine by buying the same bottle of Merlot from the supermarket week in week out. Rather, the odd dud is all part of the experience.

So, if this book gives you the confidence to 'have a go' then I will have achieved all I could have hoped for. If you try some of the wines I mention, you'll get a feel for the style of wines that float my boat. They're gutsy, spunky wines with a

INTRODUCTION

lot of character: wines that tell stories, that make me happy and help create new memories. I hope what follows makes you smile, and that the wines you discover will help carry you through life's dreadful lows and beautiful highs, and all the stuff in between.

I
First Glass

Hero bottle: *Saint-Amour, Château de Saint-Amour, Beaujolais, France*

The November sun streamed through the windows of the Eton Wine Bar, catching the specks of dust that swirled above the old reclaimed church pews we used as benches. Two hours earlier, my dad Bill and my uncle Mick had roared up in their mud-spattered Saab Turbo, triumphantly unloading cases of the precious red wine they'd just raced back home with from France. Etched on their faces was a blend of exhaustion and elation, their clothes still creased from the overnight dash. *Le Beaujolais Nouveau est arrivé!*

Now they'd lined the tall glistening-green bottles up on the bar, labels still damp from the cellars, and the lunchtime queue outside on Eton High Street buzzed with anticipation – office workers who'd escaped early, local wine merchants eager to compare notes, and regular customers who'd been coming to this annual event for years.

Then, at last, it was time to open the doors, and the throng filled the bar. Their French berets askew, Dad and Uncle Mick drew the first corks with theatrical flourish and that distinctive aroma of young wine filled the air – all crushed raspberries and youthful exuberance. Mum and Aunty Lin buzzed around with laden charcuterie boards: rough country pâtés, fat-marbled saucisson and wedges of pungent cheese.

With his first pour, Dad's eyes twinkled, while Uncle Mick, ever the showman, regaled everyone with tales of their mad race through Beaujolais backroads.

As the wines flowed, the tales grew taller, Uncle Mick and Dad got squiffier by the glass, their rich laughter like music bouncing off the walls punctuated now and then by the gentle clinking of bottles and the kissing of glasses. This wasn't just another mid-week lunch – it was Christmas come a whole month early – a celebration of tradition, adventure, and the simple pleasure of being among the first to taste the new wine of that year.

The third Thursday of November each year, Beaujolais Nouveau day, is one of my favourite dates on the calendar. It brings with it a very special type of joy. On that day, there's a carnival atmosphere in the province of Beaujolais because come midnight, wine growers across the region can release France's very first wine produced from that same year's *récoltes* (harvests). A *vin de primeur*, or early wine, this cheeky, light, violet-like red is fermented and bottled mere months after the grapes were still hanging on the vines. As such, 'serious' wine-lovers dismiss Beaujolais Nouveau as an uncouth upstart of a wine – basic and unprofound, brash and over-hyped – but, to my mind, they're missing the point entirely. To understand Beaujolais is to understand that simplicity, when done well, can also be profound.

There's something undeniably charming about the exuberant grape-juice freshness of a Beaujolais Nouveau. Light in body, bursting with fruity scents – crushed strawberry, raspberry, cherry and redcurrant – it is a red wine that is often served at a slight chill (around 12–14°C) to bring out its vitality. Uncle Mick once described it as 'tasting like someone had run a raspberry through a photocopier'; but Dad put it best, I think: 'It's the only wine that tastes better after your fourth glass than your first.' It's summer pudding in a glass, the last taste of sun as the autumn leaves fall and the air chills for the first time. A glass of a cheeky, fruity young Beaujolais refreshes both body and soul; low in tannin and gloriously gluggable, it reminds me that wine, at its heart, is made to bring pleasure.

These are wines for friendships and long lunches, for spring afternoons and autumn evenings. They pair as happily with a slice of peppery saucisson sec as they do with a carefully prepared coq au vin. Above all, they remind us that wine should bring joy to the table, make us want to reach for another glass, and make us slow down and take time to savour not just the food and drink on the table, but the moment itself. Beaujolais, like the green rolling hills it hails from, has a gentle quality to it that makes you want to linger over a glass or two just that little bit longer, so stay with me here. There's something deeply comforting about this wine, in fact: like pulling on a well-worn cashmere sweater on the first cold day of autumn. And so, Beaujolais has held a special place in our family's heart as long as I've been alive. In fact, for us it was never just about the wine, it was a culture.

When they started the business, Dad and Mick were both youngsters. Mick, in his late twenties, was the younger of the two brothers by eight years, but they were so alike they could have been identical twins. A pair of 5'10", athletically built bon vivants, their symmetrical Mediterranean complexions and easy smiles made them indistinguishable to first-time customers. They moved through the wine bar with synchronised swagger, both blessed with that natural charm that made everyone feel like an old friend. Dark-eyed and mischievous, they'd finish each other's sentences and share knowing looks across the room, their laughter as infectious as it was genuine.

Dad had been working for the old family firm, Gilbeys, which had joined others to form Independent Distillers and Vintners (IDV), which then became Grand Metropolitan. Sadly, as with many old family firms, Gilbeys didn't have a particularly strong HR department. Employ the eldest son, no matter how stupid he is, and give him way more responsibility than he can manage . . . seemed to be the policy. By the time my dad (not the eldest) went to work in what was now a huge conglomerate it was, what sounded to me, like a viper's nest and a pretty unhappy one at that. And so, when one day Dad received a letter from the firm, in which they addressed him as a number, he stuck two fingers up at their job, bought a set of chef whites and, together with his brother Mick, set up the Eton Wine Bar. Mick was wine guy and businessman and, as the chef whites allude to, Dad did the cheffing. My mum and Aunty Lin kept the wheels turning, making sure the staff and customers were happy, and the wine bar always welcoming.

The Gilbey brothers' duplicated charm but it was Mum who was the soul of the place. While Dad commanded the kitchen in his chef whites, it was Mum's cooking that we all craved; her intuitive understanding of flavour was born from pure love rather than any classical training. She knew every regular's story, held their secrets, shared their joys. She could often be found in quiet corners of the bar, consoling a disconsolate staff member, celebrating a new baby, or simply listening with that gentle smile that made everyone feel safe. Her warmth could melt the frost of a December morning.

They were an ideal partnership, though, my parents: Dad's exuberant energy balanced by Mum's nurturing presence. The wine bar was their stage, but their real magic was in creating a space where everyone felt like family. Even now, if I close my eyes, I can see them there: Dad in the kitchen in his whites, a spoon in the filling for his chicken and tarragon pie, and Mum downstairs making sure every glass was filled and every heart full.

For the four of them at the wine bar, Beaujolais was at the beating heart of it all. Their wine list read like a love letter to the region and lots of it ended up in Dad's dishes. His food was honest and rustic with a big dollop of generosity and joy, and he had an innate understanding of what flavours and ingredients worked with Beaujolais. His coq au vin, for example, had a sauce so rich it could only have been made using more vin than coq. And as for his beef cheek recipe, it guzzled more Morgon than was ever sent out to the dining room, and that's one of the more expensive wines from the region. I dread to think what the profit and loss sheet looked like!

It was therefore only fitting that Beaujolais played host to my first glass of wine. No longer a sip of Mum's on a Sunday lunch. It was a glass poured just for me, for health reasons of course – my parents were firm advocates of the health benefits of red wine in moderation. I was going to grow big and strong.

It was July 1988. I was a gangly sixteen-year-old showing too much interest in alcohol and cigarettes and, by Uncle

Mick and Dad's reckoning, I'd come of age and needed some fine tuning. So too did Mick's son, my cousin Henry, who was a year younger than me and, quite probably, Iron Maiden's number one fan. We were on a similar trajectory. The two of us, both eldest sons, were to join our dads on their annual 'buying' trip.

Dawn arrived with a firm nudge from Mum at 4 a.m., Henry and I sprawled in our respective beds – as an overnight guest, Henry's makeshift futon was hardly worthy of such a name – watching her gathering our clothes through bleary teenage eyes. Henry clutching his prized Walkman and heavy metal cassettes, we stumbled down to the kitchen to the sound of the spitting coffee machine and the smell of the fresh brew. Dad and Uncle Mick had had a few glasses the night before in excitement at their forthcoming trip and yet, even slightly hungover at 4 a.m., they still looked very much ready for the challenge ahead. Dad with his customary lumberjack look – unshaven in a thick checked shirt and threadbare brown cords – his standard uniform when not in his chef whites, whilst Mick, always a bit smarter, had donned his light-beige chinos and crisp blue shirt.

Then, as Dad and Mick continued to plot our route, Mum shepherded us all into the old battle-scarred Citroën CX, our family-car-cum-wine-delivery-vehicle, whose boot could comfortably fit ten cases of wine along with a French cash-and-carry haul filling every available void. I can remember the smell of that car still today; of the wine bar, of Dad's lasagne, and of the odd accidental spillage of red wine leftovers. It was even home to some handy emergency cooking ingredients – its very own (slightly pongy) mushroom colony growing in the passenger footwell. 'It adds character,' Dad insisted. We were heading to Beaujolais, first class.

In 1988, Beaujolais Nouveau was still the region's calling card. We, however, were bound for greater things: the home of Jean-Michel Roux, a pioneer of mobile bottling, big wig of Beaujolais, and a great pal of Uncle Mick's. (All will become clear, but for quality wine this bottling method was, and still is, a big thing in France. If you see the words '*Mis en Bouteille au Domaine / Château/Propriété*' printed either on the cork or the wine label, it's generally a sign of excellence. It means that the wine grower hasn't sent it away to the big local co-op for the final touches and bottling; instead it's all been done on-site under their watchful eye. So, Jean-Michel, genius as he was, and still is, put the bottling line on the back of a truck and drove it to the different vineyards to provide this '*mis en bouteille*' service to all those who couldn't afford to buy their own bottling line. And he got a lot of trucks in the end. Very clever!)

The small historical province of Beaujolais nestles in that sweet spot between Burgundy and the Rhône Valley. Just thirty-five miles north of Lyon, it stretches like a tipsy grin across eastern France, and for me, it is perhaps France's most disarmingly authentic region – where gnarly old vines cling to granite slopes and village bistros pay homage to the late Anthony Bourdain. On misty mornings, when the sunlight begins to stream through the café windows, carafes of local wine sit naturally alongside a plate of *jambon persillé de Bourgogne* – rustic chunks of salty ham jellied in aspic and garnished with freshly-chopped parsley – or a simple *pâté de campagne* with cornichons. The Beaujolais wine has an effortless way of making even the most modest meal feel like a celebration.

In the villages that dot this landscape, weathered stone houses overlook vineyards that have seen millennia pass by. The main grape variety you'll find here is the Gamay, which grows pretty much exclusively in Beaujolais. Other regions and countries try it but only here on these granite and schist slopes does the Gamay reach heights of magically unctuous, teeth-staining charm. And through its wines it tells stories of these mineral-rich soils it grows in.

Of course, there has always been a lot more to Beaujolais than simply the aforementioned Nouveaux. In fact, for years, Nouveaux has tainted the reputation of this wine region whose red wines are often beautifully made, food friendly and sometimes really quite fine. There are actually three quality levels in Beaujolais that are governed by the French wine laws known officially as the '*Appellation d'Origine Contrôlée*' (AOC). (For a French wine to be granted a prized AOC certification, the producer must follow strict rules in order to ensure consistency and tradition – precisely *how* and *where* the grapes are grown, and how the wine is made.)

FIRST GLASS

I like to think of the gamut of the region's wines (mostly red) as like the attendees of a French family party. First, you have the young party kids – the AC Beaujolais, which includes the youngest of the lot, Beaujolais Nouveaux; as described earlier, these are the least complex wines, with Nouveau being the baby, the first wine that France gives us every year.

Then, on the next rung on the ladder we have the groovy older cousins – the AC Beaujolais-Villages. Admittedly, a very confusing name because this appellation encompasses no specific village. Rather, it covers the good but not *great* vineyards where Gamay gives us more character and depth than in its simple, often boisterous siblings. So, basically, these Beaujolais-Villages wines are a bit like a Nouveau if it went to finishing school – it has learned to tie its shoe laces but still has bags of youthful exuberance.

So, that's two of the quality levels. The step up from that are the Crus (the classified growths) of Beaujolais. These are the villages and areas officially recognised for producing wines of exceptional quality and in Beaujolais there are ten of them. That's ten top-ranked wine-producing villages, each with their own AC, each producing their own unique slant to Beaujolais red wine made from the Gamay grape, and each allowed to put their village name on the label – Fleurie, for example – and they're the more serious party guests, the slightly snooty aunts and uncles, who insist on everyone using their full names. These wines hail from vineyards growing along a 24-kilometre strip of granite hills in the north of the region with each Cru offering an utterly charming, superior red wine, all made from the Gamay grape, each with an underlying typicity of Beaujolais, but with a subtle footprint of the parent village.

Although I just described them as snooty, actually none of these wines take themselves *too* seriously, but they reward those of us who pay attention. There is Juliénas, where I first picked grapes, which is named after Julius Caesar. Chénas and Régnié are perhaps the rarest of the Crus; Moulin-à-Vent and Morgon are the most serious, broad-shouldered of Beaujolais wines, often mistaken for the wines of Burgundy, just further north, when they're at their best: a glass of Morgon often brings the earthy comfort of autumn leaves and ripe cherries. Then there's Saint-Amour, where we were headed on this particular journey, apparently named after a soldier who founded a monastery there. Next up is Fleurie, probably the most well-known of the Crus and best thought of as the elegant sister, all violets and silk; a glass of Fleurie might remind you of iris petals and sun-warmed stone. Chiroubles sits highest of all, making Beaujolais' most ethereal wines. Côte de Brouilly and Brouilly share a hill and a name. Brouilly wraps around the base of Mont Brouilly, the mountain if you can call it that, while Côte de Brouilly clings to the steeper slopes above and looks down on its sibling with an air of superiority.

Here in Beaujolais, the *vignerons*, the vine growers and winemakers, work with a quiet pride, their fingertips stained dark purple during harvest, and their cool shaded cellars filled with the sweet-sour scent of fermentation. Here, then, you'll find humble wines. Wines that don't shout for attention. Instead, they'll pull up a chair for you, invite you to sit down, and they'll keep flowing for as long as the party lasts. They're good, honest pleasure.

The Cru wines express themselves through their 'terroir', a magical expression that is uniquely French that refers to a sense of place, the unique combination of everything that makes the grape and, therefore, the wine made from that grape all that it is – the soil it grows in, the aspect of the topography, and the climate in that specific growing season. Dad explained terroir to me as 'the reason why wine from this hill tastes different from wine from that hill, even though they're exactly the same grape and they're made in the same way by the same winemaker'. It's why a wine from Moulin-à-Vent can develop complexity for a decade or more, but one from Saint-Amour is all about its bright, youthful, charming fruit, a wine to drink young, I'd suggest within its first three years. But every bottle of Beaujolais seems to carry something of the landscape's soul – the morning mists that cling to the valleys, the warm afternoon sun on ancient stone, the gentle persistence of tradition in an ever-changing world.

Our drive across France that day was a blur of autoroute cafés, Dad's creative interpretation of French road signs, and Uncle Mick's running commentary on every vineyard we passed. 'Look boys,' he'd say, pointing at yet another hillside covered in neat echelons of vines, 'that's where real wine comes from!' Then he'd launch into a detailed explanation of every wine and gastronomic delight produced in that region. Henry was lost in his own heavy metal universe, his Walkman cranked to eleven as Bruce Dickinson wailed through the tinny headphones. Every few miles, the back of his head would connect with the Citroën's window in perfect sync with Nicko McBrain's drum solos, each thud making Dad wince into the rear-view mirror. Meanwhile, I was practically climbing into the front seat, hanging on my uncle's every word about terroir and appellations like a puppy at feeding time.

Two teenage boys, two very different journeys through France: one through the pounding rhythms of Iron Maiden, the other through the intricacies of France's 'sacred wine country'.

First up, the chalk slopes of Champagne. Then, through the ancient seabed soils of Chablis, which Mick swore you could taste in every bottle.

'This is white-wine country, boys – dry, flinty and fruity white that can develop with bottle age to give flavours of honeydew melon, marzipan and bruised apple.'

The village of Chablis is a slow two-hour drive from Burgundy proper, the Côte d'Or. The Cote d'Or lies further south and is split in two: to the north of the beautiful town of Beaune is the Côte de Nuits, famous for reds from the Pinot Noir grape; and to the south, the Côte de Beaune, famous for its whites made from Chardonnay. The region as a whole is famed for producing some of the most expensive wines in the world. And the Côte d'Or soon revealed itself, with its perfectly aligned vines on gentle slopes creeping up to dense woodland on either side. We were taking the scenic route into Beaujolais, from north to south right through its middle, cutting through every famous wine village from Chablis to Puligny Montrachet.

Here every village name has a story, we were told, as both of my pointy elbows nearly imprinted onto Dad and Mick's napes. And every slope a significance. 'That's Vosne Romanée up there,' Uncle Mick exclaimed, pointing to yet another vine-covered hillside as we passed. 'You see that little plot, that's the most expensive red wine in the world – right there, boys.' We had no hope of knowing where he was referring to and, God rest his soul, I don't think my uncle did either. I hope he was pointing to the vineyards of Domaine de La Romanée Conti.

We left the Côte d'Or in white-wine land, passing by the famous villages of Meursault, Puligny Montrachet and Chassagne Montrachet, and then the vineyards got scarcer. It was an hour or so further to reach Beaujolais. At last, as the early evening sun splattered the hills in shades of honey and gold, we rolled into Saint-Amour. Uncle Mick had run out of steam on account of his ten-hour non-stop running commentary, but Dad was still gesticulating as he climbed out of the driver's side. We were all tired and Henry's head must have been hurting from his repeatedly slamming it against the window to the beat of 'Run to the Hills'. As for me, I was exhausted. I hadn't slept for a second. But my head was fizzing with my uncle's enthusiasm, the landscape, the vines and the stories. I realise now that this was a chapter to a journey which was to shape my life forever.

Jean-Michel Roux, or JM, as we grew to call him, was exactly as I imagined a French man to look. His nose had clearly lost a few arguments and his hands had shaped themselves from countless harvests with the secateurs, but his smile lit up the whole of Beaujolais.

'*Mes amis, les Rosbifs*,' he exclaimed in his deep, hoarse roar as he hugged and kissed Dad and Uncle Mick.

Kissed them! I had told Dad very firmly at the age of eight that he couldn't kiss me anymore and now grown-ups with beards were kissing each other on both cheeks?

'*Et les petits Rosbifs*,' he hollered, then he hugged and kissed me and Henry, too!

He was a formidable man and a very successful businessman. He'd been early to the party, creating one of the first mobile wine-bottling businesses in France – Sobemab ('Société d'Embouteillage Beaujolais Mâconnais') – which went on to become one of the largest and most important bottling companies in the country.

But, although a businessman, JM was no suit. A wine-sodden version of Dad's lumberjack look: corduroy trousers, their seams stained with the grape juice of multiple harvests, as was his well-worn checked flannel shirt.

'*Bon! Une petite promenade!*' he announced as we stretched our weary limbs, his voice as deep as a wine cave, gesturing at the evening sun that hung like a ripe peach over his vineyards. JM bellowed for his son Charles but got a response from his dogs first. Deep, loud barks from the kennel we were about to pass. JM threw open the kennel door and out charged two ferocious-looking French hunting dogs the size of small ponies. Henry and I jumped back in terror, then Charles appeared, calmly garbled something to them in French which I presume translated as 'Don't eat them, yet,' then greeted us with an awkward handshake. He was around our age, a less weathered version of his father but with all the same character and mischief (I later found out), and off we set into the evening light, the air still warm from the hot June day.

This was my first vineyard walk. The vines weren't the neat garden plants I'd seen out of the window on our drive across the country. Instead, they looked more like Dad doing his stretches in the morning, gnarly and twisted with branches poking out in every direction.

JM's gesturing hands conveyed the words his English couldn't express, and Uncle Mick translated his passionate explanations: this patch of Gamay for basic Beaujolais, that slope for the Villages, and up there – he pointed to a particularly steep section – was where the Saint-Amour grew. On he gesticulated, telling stories of the frost earlier that spring and what sort of harvest they'd had the previous year.

Noses to the earth, the dogs, Arnaud and Visco, bounded ahead, tearing off at lightning speed after anything that moved, with JM bellowing after them. Charles walked beside me, pointing out things he thought might interest an English teenager – a lizard, a dead frog, and 'Let's look for a snake.'

JM paused at the top of the hill and we surveyed his mini kingdom in the golden hour. Even Henry thought this was OK. The light, the landscape, the company and the thought of dinner – this was something magical – and I began to understand why Dad and Uncle Mick had dragged us all this way.

We ambled back down through the vines, and as we approached the house, our feet dusty from the dry sandy soil, '*À table*!' came the cry from JM's wife, Françoise.

Inside, their dining room was formal, a cathedral to Frenchness, in fact. Starched white tablecloth, family silver, and three wine glasses per setting, making me wonder if we'd stumbled into a royal banquet. I was starving. We hadn't eaten since our very early motorway-service lunch and Mick had promised us great things about traditional French country cooking. 'Even better than your dad's,' he'd said.

Françoise emerged triumphant from the kitchen bearing plates piled with steaming-hot escargots, the garlic, parsley and butter sauce bubbling away like molten lava. Everyone got a bowlful apart from Henry and I, thank goodness – Henry's culinary adventures still stopped at sausages and I'd just about progressed to fish fingers, so, to us, these bubbling, garlicky snails looked like a science experiment gone wrong. And there were no chips anywhere to be seen. We were surely going to get some proper food for sixteen-year-old English boys.

Françoise sat down and JM got up from his seat to retrieve our meal. For Henry and me, it seemed, something very special was in store. Two minutes later, our host reappeared carrying two plates, each bearing the head of an enormous pike, its dead eyes staring up at our terrified faces. JM set the plates in front of each of us with no facial expression at all and sat down to continue his conversation with the adults.

I gingerly scooped up my knife and fork, tears threatening to flow, and Henry did the same, although his grasp of the cutlery looked more like that of someone holding a pitchfork. Just as I was about to pierce the pike's eyeball, JM burst into a magnificent belly laugh, stood up and ordered us to stop.

Charles looked quite composed, like he'd seen this all before, and Françoise scurried off to the kitchen to return moments later with our real dinner: fat French sausages and a generous mound of perfectly crisp pommes frites. Palpable relief all round . . . for Henry and me, because we were finally going to eat; for Dad – whose shoulders dropped about six inches – because we might finally stop sulking; same for Mick, who beamed with pride. We two unsophisticated English adolescents had faced down a French gastronomic initiation with relative dignity.

'Saint-Amour,' exclaimed JM as he grabbed a bottle off the sideboard and hurried over in my direction to fill my glass. It was like liquid rubies, the colour somewhere between summer strawberries and a blood-red sunset. The glass, thick cut crystal, threw crimson shadows across the white tablecloth and I could smell the wine as soon as it left the bottle – all crushed cherries and wild strawberries, like Mum's summer pudding. Henry's glass now filled too, this was our invitation to the wine world of Dad and Uncle Mick.

We took our first sip together, Henry and I, under JM's approving gaze and a wink from Uncle Mick. And it tasted just like my mum's summer pudding too, silky and bright, like liquid happiness and with none of the harshness of Dad's Sunday-lunch wines back home.

The warmth that spread through my chest might have been the wine, or maybe it was the pride of being treated, finally, as someone old enough to understand what made this world so magical to my dad and his brother. It was growing up and belonging. It was a door opening, one that promised excitement and joy.

These days wine from Saint-Amour is hard to come by. You're more likely to find one of the better-known Crus du Beaujolais – Fleurie, Morgon, perhaps – but I order Saint-Amour whenever I see it. I buy it to transport me back to that dining room, to JM's laughter, to the plate of escargots, the pike's head with its beady eye, and those delicious fat sausages. I savour it to remember that night when wine became *my* thing, not just my dad's. It's a story, my story, that started with the painfully early wake up and is still going, the starter gun having been fired with that very first glass of Saint-Amour.

We've grown up like brothers, Henry and me. In separate houses with different parents but both with two powerful influences in our lives: wine and the wine bar from our parents, and fishing from our paternal grandmother Maureen. Despite her best efforts, my interest in fishing stalled at the age of eight. She'd taken Henry and me on holiday to Scotland and given us each our own fishing rod. I ended up throwing mine in the loch on its first outing then got so cross with Henry laughing at me I threw him in too. He's gone on to forge a brilliant career in fishing but he's still a 'Diet Coke and sausages' man, who finds Iron Maiden a great deal more compelling than wine, while I've gone full throttle wine.

And for me, that trip to Beaujolais was the beginning of my lifelong love affair, and what a wine to start with – light, fruity and easy. A Saint-Amour that tantalised my tongue rather than marched through my mouth. I'd got the wine bug and I'd go on to weave it into every bit of my life – my university degree included.

By the time we returned home to Waltham Saint Lawrence, I was hooked. Our tour to Beaujolais had gotten me fascinated in all that goes into making wine and it made me to want to discover more. Getting to know more about different grape varieties was quite an important part of it, and so I learned that the Pinot Noir variety comes from Burgundy and packs more of a punch than Beaujolais' Gamay grape. If Saint-Amour was a summer pudding, a glass of Pinot Noir (provided it came from a good Burgundy village, Volnay perhaps) was more autumn berries – still plenty of red fruit but with more depth and complexity to the wine. I'd search for savoury notes and I'd find them. Sometimes meaty, sometimes mushroomy, and sometimes the smell of the woods just beyond my back garden after it's been raining, like the smell of a forest floor (I think they call it petrichor) – yes, it's incredible, you really can get these smells and senses from fermented grape juice! Such wines were expensive and tasted as such – like silk gliding across my tongue. I was lucky enough to try them when Mum and Dad brought the odd bottle home.

I tasted and grew to love Cabernet Sauvignon back then too. This is a red wine grape variety that's grown all over the world but its native home is south-western France, Bordeaux and, more specifically, the Médoc, the world-famous wine region to the north of Bordeaux city. Cabernet takes the intensity up a notch; on my first sip, it grabbed me by my lapels rather than kissing me on both cheeks. And then I found Merlot, a softer, gentler grape, more a hug than a punch, which in Bordeaux they often blend with Cabernet. Merlot makes another of France's most expensive wines, Pomerol, more specifically, Château Petrus. Both Merlot and Cabernet, I discovered, have the backbone to sit comfortably with the steak that Mum occasionally brought home from the wine bar for our Saturday dinner – a real treat and one of my treasured family memories.

Between the poles of Cabernet Sauvignon and Pinot Noir lies a whole spectrum of red grape varieties. Syrah, the deep, dark grape whose origin is the Northern Rhône, is considered one of the noble red grape varieties (capable of making intense, profound and extremely fine wines) and it always brings black pepper and spice to the party. The ancient Italian Sangiovese delivers rusticity and elegance to the wines of Tuscany while Tempranillo, a native of Spain and the main player in Rioja, carries hints of leather, cinnamon and tobacco. And then, of course, winemakers will go and blend these varietals too, mixing pepper with tobacco, cinnamon with blackcurrant. It's a never-ending voyage of sensual discovery.

It's Cabernet Sauvignon that double hooked me, though.

Its wines hit the glass like black velvet, deep and dark as a midwinter night and much darker than Pinot Noir. A Cabernet Sauvignon demands attention and oozes confidence. The first smell – blackcurrant – is sometimes sprinkled with a dusting of cedar, tobacco and, if you're drinking one from Bordeaux, maybe leather. You could also find hints of pepper, black cherries, plums and sometimes, if you're drinking a Cab from Australia, a whisper of mint or eucalyptus, too, to freshen the whole experience. This is a majestic grape, capable of sucking flavour out of the soil as few others can, whose wine, in youth, can be as structured as a Victorian mansion with firm, austere tannins. But, with a bit of maturity, it gains elegance and complexity, like a well-maintained vintage BMW, with each passing year. The best examples, whether from Bordeaux, California or Australia, carry themselves with assured grace and unfold in the glass like a well-crafted story. They're wines of substance and nobility, power and persistence, a liquid reminder that sometimes life is better with the volume turned down.

Cabernet Sauvignon is a wine that loves food too. It sings its best tune with a delicious cut of beef, and it can transform a simple Bolognese sauce into a symphony of warm content. I discovered this when I was tasked with cooking my first 'house dinner' at uni in Oxford – well, to be clear, Oxford Polytechnic, soon to be rechristened Oxford Brookes University. It was 1992, I was a twenty-year-old Geography and History student, living with two of my worst behaved school friends in a tiny rented house in Jericho, right by the Oxford canal.

Even then as the archetypal impoverished student, I had wine on my mind. Wine grabbed me in a way that beer, spirits, or drugs never could – not for the buzz, but for its ability to tell stories of time and place. I'd daydream mid-lecture about vineyards and soil types, but I wasn't the only geek in town. There were others with similar obsessions to me, like Oliver, enrolled in History of Art but as obsessed with clocks as I was with wine. Both of us loved our subject for its ability to tell stories of time (excuse the pun) and place, and whilst it didn't make us the coolest guys on the beat, it gave us the common ground to become very good friends. Together, we were the happy nerds of our university pack.

With my reputation for wine came an expectation for cooking and it wasn't long before my two housemates suggested a cooking rota, with me going first. Little did they know it but my cooking repertoire began and ended at spaghetti Bolognese, which I was sure I could conjure into a meal of warmth and contentment. It was probably less cooking and more murdering some cheap mince with a couple of tins of tomatoes, but at the time I thought I was Marco Pierre White and, well, Marco wouldn't serve plonk, even if his budget was a mere £3.99.

Back then, I was most familiar with the local Sainsbury's wine selection. I would browse its fairly sparse shelves – predominantly French back then, and with very few helpful signposts on how to choose a winner. There were no tasting notes, starred shelf labels, or sweetness charts as we see in wine aisles today, just bottles and prices. And in those days, there were no search engines either. This was the early nineties, so I couldn't look these wines up on my phone.

I'd been weaned on Dad and Uncle Mick's Beaujolais, of course, along with other French classics like Muscadet, a searingly fresh, zippy white wine from north-western France; and

Corbières, a rustic, full-bodied, tannic red from Languedoc-Roussillon in the deep south. Others too, some of which were so questionable I'd tried them just the once, but even then I recognised many of the labels. I'd thumbed through my growing collection of wine books – the encyclopaedic *Hugh Johnson's Wine Companion*; Oz Clarke's *Wines of the New World*; Jancis Robinson's *Oxford Companion to Wine*, to highlight just three – so I knew about a few of the great grape varieties that carry a distinctive fruit flavour wherever they grow (I'll touch on these as we go), and I'd even tasted some of them before. But those wines tended to be *really* expensive. So, I'd either know or look up the grape varieties of the French wines I liked, then play 'hunt down the cheap equivalents'. Want the blackberries from a Bordeaux? Go for a Cabernet Sauvignon. Strawberries from a Burgundy? Plump for a Pinot Noir. Gooseberries from a Sancerre? Select a Sauvignon Blanc.

So, I stood there staring at the Sainsbury's shelves – just me and the smattering of knowledge gleaned from my well-thumbed books. Anyway, I picked up a bottle, read the label on the back, then put it back down. Plucked another off the shelf and did the same. And so on. This laborious process continued while a woman next to me confidently swept down to get her bottle of Chianti . . . but I wanted blackberries in *my* bottle. And I found one, a good one and it was just about manageable on my student budget. I could even afford two: one for us and one for the sauce pot.

It was four years since the Iron Curtain had come down and the supermarket wine shelves were littered with great value offerings from the former Communist bloc: Bulgarian Cabernet Sauvignon; Romanian Pinot Noir; and a

Hungarian wine called Bull's Blood which, it seemed to me, had every red grape variety known to man in the mix. That night, it was the Bulgarian Cabernet Sauvignon for us. The label illustration featured an imposing castle with gothic writing underneath. Although it looked like it could have been Dracula's house red, it was a Cabernet Sauvignon, and that's exactly what I was after. I'd heard Dad refer to it as his favourite wine and grape, and whilst it was a pound more expensive than the wines all of my friends would bring to our student house parties, the fact that Dad loved it (well, maybe not *this* precise bottle) was my guarantee of satisfaction.

The man at the checkout didn't seem to appreciate the gravitas of the moment. He didn't even raise an eyebrow, even to ask for my ID, let alone acknowledge my sophisticated choice. He beeped my prized Bulgarian Cabernet Sauvignon through along with my budget mince, own-brand spaghetti, chopped tinned tomatoes, onion and garlic like it was a bottle of Vimto. Part of me wanted to stop him to explain why I'd chosen the Cabernet Sauvignon but thankfully I thought better of it.

Our student house in Combe Road was a testament to three recent school leavers who still thought bath towels dried on the floor. The yellowed curtains had witnessed every cultural shift since the Boer War and in my ground-floor bedroom – formerly known as the 'front room' – the windows looked out onto a grown-up world. We were the only students living on this road, sharing it with lovely young families who thought we were anything but.

Behind my room lurked the kitchen. Well, it was actually more like a refuse centre, each greasy laminate surface carrying scars from the toastie machine and remnants of the last night/week's kebabs. That had been the extent of our culinary enterprise thus far, so I hoped my efforts would be the start of great changes to come.

Before my crusade of cleanliness that afternoon, it had been a place where food went to retire and where plastic containers full of decomposing matter doubled as biology projects. The fridge was its very own ecosystem and the sink a fertile culture-incubator, but tonight the place was sluiced and disinfected. And, armed with Dad's heavily abridged Bolognese recipe, and two bottles of Bulgarian Cabernet Sauvignon, I was ready and set to create a right royal feast.

I opened one of my bottles for 'cooking wine' purposes, though at least half of it found its way down my throat instead. The late celebrity TV chef, Keith Floyd, was my inspiration here, a flamboyant feature of late eighties and nineties British telly, always cooking with wine, often more than a little sozzled, and always brashly funny. (In fact, by the end it seemed he couldn't cook a dish well unless he had at least half a bottle of wine inside him.) As for me, the other half of the Bulgarian red did find its way into my meat sauce, although much of that somehow ended up splattered across the murky-white laminate surfaces and up the back of the oven.

Yes, its creation was quite chaotic but my first student Bolognese was, as my housemates agreed, utterly delicious. The sauce had developed the kind of depth that only comes from getting slightly distracted and letting things caramelise a touch too long – the slightly-burnt bits adding a richness that was definitely not mentioned in Dad's recipe. The mysterious herbs, unlabelled at the back of the cupboard, had contributed their very own bit of magic and the wine, it must have been the wine, gave the mince a depth of flavour that I was proud of. We ate like kings that night. Kings who used chipped, mismatched plates and drank red wine from two water glasses and an old jam jar.

The wine was special too. A magnificently deep purple-black colour with the body to match, it had all the subtlety of a Soviet-era tractor. Power over finesse. Its first sniff was memorable, oozing baked black fruits, the kind that had over-ripened too long in the sun. I searched for Dad and Uncle Mick's tones of tobacco and cedar, but instead I got my housemate Markus's cigarette smoke – in those days everybody still smoked indoors. It grew on me though, once the fruit had found its way through. It had big burly shoulders of blackberries and blackcurrants, tannins that wrapped around my entire tongue, but there was a ripeness to it that made everything . . . OK . . . in the end.

I kept those empty bottles for ages – my first 'real' wine purchase. They sat on our kitchen windowsill among the empty vodka bottles and rancid washing-up cloths until someone stuck candles in their tops and plonked them on the kitchen table. Every time I looked at them, I felt like I'd come of age.

HOW WINE IS MADE

Now is probably the right time to talk about how this amazing liquid is made. So many people have explained the basic process and principles, and I'm regularly surprised at how often something so simple can be made to sound so complicated. So, here goes:

1. **IT STARTS WITH GRAPES.** Not your ordinary table/dessert grapes though, the kind we see on the supermarket shelves. These are grape varieties from vines called *Vitis vinifera*, cultivated specifically for making wine. The fruit is normally smaller than your regular table grape and not nearly as tasty to eat – they often have thicker skins packed with colour and flavour, and the flesh is higher in acids and all the other chemical components that make wine so delicious.

2. **HARVEST** begins when the fruit is ripe, in late summer/autumn – February/March for the Southern Hemisphere; August/September for the Northern Hemisphere.

3. **WHITE WINE** is made from grapes with green skins (but we call them white). The winemaker crushes the grapes, presses out the juice (called 'must'), and then adds yeast. Yes, you can use the yeast that is naturally there on the skins of grapes and in the vineyard but most wineries use commercial yeast that they know will get the job done. The job is to eat the sugar in the grape juice and turn it into alcohol. The more sugar in the juice, the higher the alcohol content of the finished wine.

4. **RED WINE** gets its colour from the skins of the black/red grape varieties. To make red wine, the winemaker crushes

the grapes – the skins, the pips, and sometimes even the stalks go in with the must (grape juice) – then, in goes the yeast (if more is needed) and fermentation completes before pressing out the juice, usually about fourteen days or so later.

5. **WHITE WINES FROM BLACK GRAPES** is a thing. Weirdly enough, the juice of black grapes is white, which is why you can make white wine (Champagne is a classic example) using Pinot Noir (a black grape).

6. **ROSÉ WINE** is like making white wine but from black/red grapes. The winemaker crushes the whole grapes, allowing the juice to macerate with the skins for only a few hours (maybe three to six hours for a coral pink colour), then, when it has reached just the right level of pinkness, the crushed grape mixture is pressed and fermented as for a white wine.

7. **ORANGE WINE** is the funky one, which we are seeing more and more these days in the cool city wine bars and restaurants. This is wine made from white grapes but using a 'skin contact fermentation' – so the grape juice is left to macerate and ferment in contact with the skins – for anything from a day to several months – to give it structure and a richer mouthfeel. It's a bit like a white wine made like a red.

8. **SPARKLING WINE** can be made in a few ways. The best ones, e.g. Champagne, are made by adding yeast and a sugar solution to a still wine with a low alcohol content (11^0), which is then bottled, then sealed with a crown cap. This starter wine is called the base wine. The yeast then eats the sugar, releasing CO_2 and turning the sugar into a bit more

alcohol. The yeast dies when it's eaten all the sugar and we're left with a bottle of beautiful sparkling fizz. There's then the popular option of disgorging the wine to get the yeast out. Prosecco is fermented in a pressurised tank.

9. THE WINERY and winemaking process can have a huge impact on the flavour of wine – the type of vessel the juice is fermented in, the temperature, what yeasts are used, any filtration (which can strip flavour), etc., etc. So winemaking is not just about the grape. (But there's no need to get bogged down yet!)

10. QUALITY WINE is always trying to convey a sense of place as well as grape variety. The French refer to this as 'terroir', which is the magic combination of the grape grown in that particular soil and in that particular climate. Terroir is that elusive 'something' winemakers all over the world are striving for.

Wine Wanker Approved List #1:
Ten Favourite Light Reds – Chillable & Chuggable

(**Hero bottle** – *Saint-Amour, Château de Saint-Amour, Beaujolais, France*)

Saumur Champigny, Château Yvonne, Parnay, France
Dad used to love Cabernet Franc from the Loire. He described it as a wine with energy, pure fruit and class. This was the first Cabernet Franc I drank and it was like biting into the juiciest, freshest, ripest plum I'd ever had.

Fleurie, Domaine Michel Chignard, Beaujolais, France
Uncle Mick loved this elegant Beaujolais Cru wine so much he named his dog after it. It's made from 100 per cent Gamay grapes and whilst Fleurie is often the lightest, most sophisticated and feminine style of the Beaujolais Crus, Chignard adds plenty of plushness and richness to it . . . which is absolutely alright by me.

Pinot Noir, The Main Divide, Canterbury, New Zealand
This is such a juicy and delicious NZ Pinot. It's so ripe and generous while still offering the finesse and elegance I love from Pinot Noir. I really don't think Burgundy winemakers can get anywhere near the joyful chuggability of this wine at this money – it's terrific!

Saint-Amour 'Le Clos du Chapitre', Domaine Chardigny, Leynes, France
This wine comes from the exact Clos (walled area) where my dad and Mick's great friends, Jean-Michel and Francoise, live.

Light, elegant and brimming with cranberry-like fruit, this is one of the most joyful wines I've ever drunk.

Chiroubles, Domaine Emile Cheysson, Beaujolais, France
This is a red Beaujolais Cru and perhaps the most delicious I've ever tasted. Though I had always been told that Beaujolais should be drunk young, I remember tasting a bottle that was ten years old, and it was as good, if not better, than a £30 Beaune Premier Cru from the heart of Burgundy.

Fleurie La Madone, La Reine de l'Arenite (Boutinot), Beaujolais, France
'La Madone' is the most noteworthy '*climat*' (specific area) within the AOC of Fleurie. The wines from here are all crushed berries and flowers – so pretty and elegant – the sort that will always make you (well certainly me) smile. I had my first taste of Fleurie 'La Madone', slightly chilled, in the summer of '95 and completely LOVED it.

Les Gravilices Saint Nicolas de Bourgueil, Domaine Amirault, Loire, France
This is a really grown up, lively, punchy Cabernet Franc from the Loire Valley. It's fresh and generously fruity. All of Xavier Amirault's wines tell a story. They're packed with character and I'm a big fan.

Valpolicella Classico, Allegrini, Valpolicella, Italy
Made from the Corvina grape variety, this is a soft, juicy, easy-drinking style of wine made by one of the kings of the region. The tannins are so soft, almost imperceptible, and the fruit is rich and ripe.

Frappato, 'Rina Russa', Santa Tresa, Sicily
Sicily's answer to Beaujolais. This wine is light and full of energy and vitality. It's liquidised strawberries in a glass. I'm picturing a summer picnic now as I write.

Barbera d'Alba 'La Gemella', Viberti Giovanni, Barolo, Italy
Barbera is a terrific grape to enjoy cool. This is full of juicy blueberry fruit with minimal tannin and refreshing acidity.

2
Wine Work

BROKENWOOD

semillon

750 ml   WINE OF AUSTRALIA   11.5% VOL

Hero bottle: *Brokenwood Hunter Valley Semillon, New South Wales, Australia*

September 1990, I was back for my second visit to the Beaujolais and it wasn't exactly the sun-drenched French idyll I remembered. I'd left school earlier that June, had a three-month celebration in various bars and pubs, then headed out to France to find out more about grapes. I was to work the harvest in the region I knew best, to see the business end of wine.

So, there I joined thirty grape pickers from all corners of the world: Brits, Irish, Aussies, Polish, Swedes, Germans and more. But instead of basking in the late-summer heat, it seemed that the rain did not stop the entire fortnight I was there and so, soaked to the bone, each day from dawn to nightfall, we sloshed through the vineyards of Fleurie and Juliénas.

The family I was working for, the Perachons, was as typically French as I'd ever encountered. My boss was the son, Laurent, a kindly man in his early thirties who maintained a Gallic optimism in spite of all of the downpours and, especially, my ineptitude. For this fresh-faced English school leaver, the work of grape-picking was a comedy of errors. As the seasoned pickers moved efficiently along their rows of vines, I fumbled with my secateurs like a drunk sommelier with a corkscrew. The first bunch of grapes I harvested looked like they'd been in a bar brawl, but slowly I improved and Laurent would pass by, inspect my work and smile a little more each time.

Each evening, Madame Perachon's hearty cooking transformed we thirty tired workers into fully-fledged party animals and the barn where we ate became our nightly festival tent. The long trestle tables groaning with food, wine flowing as freely as the rain outside, we'd drink from any glass we could find or straight from jugs full of the previous year's vintage. With each glass our French got better and our singing got worse.

I learned more about winemaking in those two weeks than I could from any tome of reference – how to stay upright on a muddy vineyard slope while carrying a heavy basket of grapes; how to avoid wasps who'd developed a taste for grape juice; and when to call a halt in the evenings so I could function the next day. And I learned so much about grapes and the vineyards. The fruit sorting table became my classroom. I learned that making great wine starts with ruthless rejection: green grapes that are meant to be red, rotten grapes, leaves, spiders, the occasional startled lizard – all had to be picked out and jettisoned before only the very best grapes could begin their journey to become Fleurie or Juliénas. And by the end of those two weeks, I also understood that wine isn't just made – it's grown. Healthy grapes, of which I didn't think we had many, make good wine.

It still amazes me how the grape – that small, seemingly simple fruit – holds the secret to everything we can taste in a bottle. I touched on this earlier but these wine grape varieties are miles apart from our table grapes, the sort that sit in plastic containers on the supermarket shelves. The grapes I'm talking about here, *Vitis vinifera*, are their grown-up cousins. Unlike regular dessert and table grapes, they hang from the vine in smaller clusters, each berry barely the size of a blueberry, with their skins often dusted with a waxy bloom.

Taste one of these grapes straight from the vine and you'll understand why they are never going to make it into the fruit bowl. They're intense, with thick, chewy skins. They look pretty uninviting actually. Bite into one and it almost fights back – exploding before you've even pierced the skin. These are berries with a tartness and wild energy that makes your mouth dance and pucker, each one packed with the building blocks of the wine-to-be.

Walking down the vine rows, you can see the difference too. These vines aren't the sort you'd find in a show garden. They're disciplined, like soldiers, each one shaped by decades of careful pruning. Their leaves are small, their wood gnarled, everything about them suggests that they haven't come for a beauty contest.

Each of those berries I was harvesting was its own little miracle of chemistry. Made with sunlight, soil and rain, all delivered by the vines to each individual ripening fruit, it would soon become something so much more profound than just grape juice. Here I tasted first-hand how two grapes, exactly the same but grown just a kilometre or two apart, could taste so different.

In my mind, the grape is the king of fruits, performing tricks that no rival can match, transforming itself into an endless parade of unrelated aromas and flavours. Each small grape can be read like the diary of its growing season, telling of spring rains, the summer heat and the morning mists, not simply capturing flavours but more like inventing them, magicking up notes that go way beyond just fruit – think leather, tobacco, chocolate and coffee. Grapes, in short, are nature's flavour grenades, the skins, the flesh, the pulp and the pips, just waiting for yeast to pull the pin.

Other fruits stand steadfast when fermented. Perry, no matter how much it tries, still tastes of pears, and an apple cider still tastes of apples. (Only Muscat, the most stubborn of all grapes, manages to hold its identity through fermentation. A bit like Jack Black: completely unique and (thankfully) he's always Jack Black in every movie he makes.) Mostly, though, grapes are like an impossibly talented, slightly irritating friend who excels effortlessly at everything – while the rest of the fruit bowl is content playing one note, grapes go out there and smash out complete symphonies.

And give the same grape a different postcode and it gives us an entirely different story. For example, take the Sauvignon Blanc grapes growing in Sancerre, one of my favourite regions, which sits perched overlooking the Loire river in central northern France. The Sancerre vineyards roll down limestone and chalk slopes to the valley floor and so here the grapes somehow turn the sunlight and soil into fresh-cut grass, gooseberry and elderflower. The very same Sauvignon Blanc grape, however, when taken to the sunny slopes of Marlborough in New Zealand, becomes something entirely different – a tropical carnival of mango and passionfruit.

Chardonnay is equally puzzling. In Chablis, just to the south-east of Sancerre, its language is lemon and mineral, with a slight marzipan accent. But take it to the Napa Valley in California and the grape becomes a different wine entirely – all tropical fruit, butter and pineapple ripeness.

WINE WORK

Then there's Syrah, another one of my favourite grapes and sometimes, confusingly, labelled as Shiraz. In a glass of Cornas from the Northern Rhône, it conjures up freshly cracked black pepper, so expressive it will have you looking for the pepper mill behind the bottle. There's no black pepper anywhere near the region of Cornas, nor in any Syrah or Shiraz grape, but it somehow finds its way through, like a master perfumer who's managing to do it with just sunlight, soil and weather.

But back to that late summer of 1990. I returned from working the *vendange* (grape harvest) in Beaujolais to start three months' work at the family wine bar. By the following January, I had saved enough money to buy myself a round-the-world plane ticket. I set off with my old school friend and great travelling pal, Nick, and after a quick jaunt through Malaysia, Hong Kong and Indonesia, we arrived in Australia. Alas, we'd used up all our savings in Indonesia so to fund our ongoing travels, industrious fellows that we were, we each got jobs. Within two months we had enough money to buy a car, an old Chrysler Station Wagon, our chariot all the way up to Queensland – destination, Cape Tribulation, near the top of the East Coast. The front seat was like one long leather, well actually plastic, sofa, big enough to fit three, and the boot could house a small village. The gear shift poked out of the steering column and had three promising options for forward propulsion. First gear sounded like the door was being ripped off its hinges; second gear was like we were dropping anchor; and third gear – when we eventually coaxed the old girl into submission – hummed.

As we drove north I confess, at this time in my life, I was perhaps most motivated by getting on the beers with Nick.

But a call home to Mum and Dad a couple of days before we left Sydney had put paid to that plan. While I was jabbering away to Mum, Dad had got his map out and he worked out that we'd be driving straight through the Hunter Valley. It was Australia's oldest wine region and the largest in New South Wales, he told me.

'You must stop there, Tom. You can't go all the way to the other side of the world and not experience Australia's sensational wine culture. I'll fix you a couple of visits,' he insisted.

To be frank, our experience of Sydney had so far been limited to various bars and bottle shops and so I wasn't convinced that Australia *had* any wine culture. But this diversion was sure to take my mind off the reading list from Oxford Polytechnic, with which I wasn't getting on very well. So, there I was, on the other side of the world, about to find out how they did winemaking upside down.

The Hunter Valley is mostly about growing Semillon, one of wine's great shape-shifter grapes that can perform magic tricks in the bottle. When it's young, its wine is like liquid sunlight – pale, translucent, but with an intensity that can catch you off guard. It has an acidity that crackles like electricity, all citrus zest and green apples. Getting older and more mature, the citrus turns to preserved lemon and lime – almost marmaladey, with hints of honey; not sweet but complex, and yet it still keeps its freshness. Even at twenty or thirty years old, Hunter Semillon keeps that vibrant core of acidity. It's Australia's gift to the wine world – one of the very few white wines that can age as long as reds, and it costs a fraction of the price of some of the fine French white and red wines. (These days, top-flight Aussie Semillon goes for around £40 a bottle in the UK.)

In Sydney, Nick and I had teamed up with two other school friends, Crispin and Johnny, and they were going to tag along with us up to Queensland. Of the four of us, if Nick was the tearaway and most likely to get us into scrapes, Johnny was the sensible one. Now he's a management consultant and, in hindsight, was always going to be a sensible management consultant. Nick, meanwhile, has built a pub empire. Always in and around the bar either with, or as, the biggest character in the room. Curly-headed Crispin was the joker of our pack and a dead-ringer for Dennis the Menace from the *Beano*. Johnny and Crispin seemed to be having a similar Australian cultural experience to us, i.e. hours spent in various bars. Once packed, an old mattress laid out in the boot (my and Nick's sleeping quarters), we hit the road. Our old Chrysler Station Wagon cruised along the Pacific Highway like a well-fed whale, our progress marked by a squeaking suspension and the odd thud from somewhere under the bonnet. Nick was driving, I was map-reader, while Crispin and Johnny lolled about like kings in the back.

On our first evening we found a campsite just as the Chrysler's temperature gauge was creeping towards red. She announced our arrival with a medley of her greatest hits – a screech of brakes, the squeaking and rattling suspension, and a knock from under the bonnet as the engine was put to rest for the night.

When dawn broke the next day, the Hunter Valley sprawled before us, all vineyards and possibilities, the morning mist still clinging to the vines. We were four young English lads let loose in Australia's oldest wine region, armed with nothing but a dog-eared Lonely Planet guide. Until, that was, I laid my hands on a local wine guide in the campsite shop. Yes, that prod from Dad had soon reignited my need for a bit of purpose and some intrigue about our destination. I scribbled some notes in the margins, prepared just enough to hope that we might not come across as oafish and unappreciative Poms, and we were off.

My friends knew my mum and dad well. They knew about the wine bar: that Dad was a chef and that they imported their own wine. Also, I was the only one among us who could pronounce 'Châteauneuf du Pape' without sounding like I was having a stroke so, naturally, I was the designated 'wine expert' in our motley crew. Nick, Crispin and strait-laced Johnny, meanwhile, viewed the whole outing as an opportunity to guzzle as much free booze as possible – an excuse to get blotto. Honestly, it was like taking three hyperactive puppies to an antiques shop with the designated 'expert' nearly as excited as his litter.

Dad had fixed us a meeting at Brokenwood Wines, one of the top producers in the Hunter. This was everything I'd imagined a contemporary Australian winery should be – a grand state-of-the art exhibition of innovation and tradition wrapped in weathered wooden verandas, surrounded by lush green vineyards rolling away out of view.

Claire, our host, greeted us with a measured smile. Her eyes flickered briefly to our slightly lived-in appearance (sleeping in a Chrysler doesn't help one to look, or smell, one's freshest) but then her Aussie hospitality won out and our tour began. She was, as we were to find out, a complete charmer who wasn't going to let us leave without having picked up a bit of knowledge.

The morning sun was warm. Out among the vines it smelt like a herb garden and I was hanging on her every word – she was explaining things in a way I hadn't heard before – soil composition, vine training methods, the lot. Meanwhile Nick was discovering that vine rows make excellent bowling alleys for rocks and stones.

It was a brief tour and as we made our way back to the Cellar Door, the tasting room, enthusiasm amongst the team grew. Then, just as we'd walked through the door, Crispin announced to all and sundry that I was 'English wine royalty'.

'His dad owns half the wine in England,' he proclaimed. Poor Claire looked puzzled whilst I blushed and tried to give Crispin a good kick. Dad was 'just a chef' who'd kindly organised this visit for us via one of her colleagues, I explained, and that's when the penny seemed to drop.

'Hang on a sec – you're those lot from Windsor Castle, aren't ya? Your dad's the one cooking for the royals and that?'

I explained that she was about half-a-mile out but she'd got the gist of it and suddenly the mood changed. I, at least, was being taken seriously. She was now bombarding me with the full-on nerd facts, which I revelled in whilst nodding along sagely, trying not to panic about whether 'Semillon' was spelt with one 'l' or two.

Crispin, the joker, was struggling to concentrate. I noticed, out of the corner of my eye, that he'd moved on to his own special brand of entertainment – turning the spittoon into a basketball hoop. And even sensible Johnny was having an uncharacteristically naughty day. He was quite clearly swallowing rather than spitting during the tasting, and now was asking all about Australian 'proper beer'. And Nick, the naughtiest of us all by quite some shot, was getting more and more pissed, and louder and louder, exclaiming that everything tasted exactly 'like wine', and getting more excited about this with every glass.

Things took a turn for the worse at wine number four – a Shiraz that Claire described as having 'notes of black pepper and leather'. Johnny, who by now had given up any pretence of spitting, announced that it smelled exactly like his dad's hiking boots. Crispin found this so hilarious he sprayed his mouthful of red wine across the tasting room counter. I went to clean it up but only ended up knocking over an entire flight of wine glasses. And then something very unexpected happened – somewhere between Crispin's impromptu showering of the tasting counter and Nick's questions on why Brokenwood's wine labels didn't have pictures on 'like beer does', something magical was set in motion. Instead of throwing in the towel (which she absolutely should have done), Claire started to teach us about wine, properly teach us, as if she'd recognised that behind this monkey business, all of us were actually quite interested to learn, not just me. And this despite Nick trying to sabrage a bottle of fizz with his flip flop, an unorthodox technique I've never seen covered in any wine course.

Undaunted, Claire poured us a glass of one of their very best Semillons.

'Give this one a burl,' she said, looking confident that it would stun us into silence.

That first sip was a revelation, an epiphany in a glass. I'd never tasted the Semillon grape in the form of a dry white wine before (in Bordeaux it makes the most amazing sweet white wines and some dry whites, too), and this was all honeysuckle, toast and lemon curd and yet somehow, still bone-dry and fresh as a daisy. This was everything Dad had tried to teach me about wine's ability to tell stories, captured in a single glass of aged Hunter Semillon.

We bought a bottle of that Semillon. It cost about half of our remaining travel budget and for the price we could have bought three nights' worth of boxed wine from the local bottle shop, so my companions were reluctant. But this was the tax they had to pay to keep me happy. And that bottle from Brokenwood Wines became something of a legend on our trip. It made us feel special and we carried it around for weeks, treating it with the kind of reverence usually reserved for your grandmother's wedding ring or some precious religious artifact.

Finally, we drank it together on our way back down the coast, on a beach in Byron Bay. The four of us sitting in relative silence, savouring every mouthful, listening to the waves rolling in, watching the sun disappear over the horizon. Not an easy moment to forget. I'd discovered that great wine can be made outside of France and I was hungry to find out more.

But I had some studies to finish first. How the heck was I going to shoehorn wine into a degree in History and Geography? Well, I did, wherever I could. With a few friends we set up a wine society (aptly christened the 'Dead Brains' Society'). Together, we tasted whatever we could, whenever we could get hold of a bottle. Oxford's dreaming spires might have been dozing in the afternoon sun but I was conducting my own research in Oddbins on the High Street, working my way through their inventory with far more gusto than I ever put into my coursework. I took on a weekend-manager role back in the Eton Wine Bar, tasting any dribbles left in bottles on tables. And during uni holidays I travelled as much as I could afford, to see whatever wine-growing region I could get to.

Eventually, in 1993, towards the end of my three-year course, I had to dream up a subject for my dissertation. One morning, an idea came to me like a cork flying out of a very frisky bottle of Champagne. What's something that's been around since Roman times, that lives or dies depending on climate, weather, and all things geography? Wine, of course. So, for the title of my dissertation, how about 'The History of English Wine and its Potential with Global Warming'? My tutor greeted the suggestion in the same way she might had the moon landed in her back garden.

Back then in the early nineties, any mention of English wine was greeted with looks that questioned how long I'd been let out of the asylum. English and Welsh vineyards were but a patchwork of hopefulness, planted with grape varieties with weird names that sounded more like German railway stations than fruit: Müller-Thurgau, Reichensteiner and Ortega, to list just three. But, in a country more famous for drinking it and trading it than making it, idealistic wannabe wine growers had planted them because they were about the only grapes that had any hope of ripening in our dreadful summers.

The exception here is a vineyard called Nyetimber in West Sussex. The team there had seen the opportunity early and, in 1988, had planted the Champagne grape varietals Chardonnay, Pinot Noir and Pinot Meunier, and today are one of our very best producers of fine sparkling wine. In those days, though, they were still a quiet voice crying in the wilderness.

The story of how we got here, from those early days of English wine to today, in some ways might mirror my own path in wine – from that first discovery of Hunter Valley Semillon to understanding and appreciating why English wine is so good today. Like that aged Semillon in the Hunter, some things only make sense in their proper place and so, those German railway-station grape varieties that once filled English vineyards were stepping stones, I guess, necessary experiments following Nyetimber on the path to finding our true vinous voice.

To research my dissertation, armed with my Ordnance Survey maps, I set off to discover England's viticultural secrets in Mozza, my sky-blue Morris Minor. Starting Mozza's engine was more of a suggestion than a certainty; the crank handle that replaced the car key was less a backup and more a daily necessity; and the heater operated by opposites – hot air in summer, arctic blasts in winter. Oh, and if it was raining, the heating system welcomed that in too. Getting Mozza going on cold mornings involved rolling her down the hill, diving into the driver's seat 25 metres before the traffic lights, and then performing a complicated ballet involving gear shift, clutch and brakes – aka a bump start. I'd beefed up the in-car entertainment with a stereo system fit for a Ferrari. It needed to be so to hear anything above the roar, if it was a roar, of Mozza's engine. CDs were strewn all over the passenger seat and the footwell – U2's albums *Achtung Baby* and *The Joshua Tree* were hot favourites at the time. Primal Scream's *Screamadelica* got a good airing, too, interspersed with significant splatterings from Queen, Simple Minds and Tears for Fears.

When I eventually reached them, the vineyard owners I found were a magnificent bunch of real English eccentrics who would talk about soil type and aspect like they were the only ones in the world who knew anything about growing grapes; quite happy with their leaking roof as long as they had a bottle of their delicious Müller-Thurgau white wine in hand. These were eternal optimists who'd decided that if England could grow turnips, we could surely manage to produce sufficient grapes to make a few decent bottles of wine.

My first visit was to a retired major in Kent, whose greeting having spotted me stepping out of Mozza was, 'Never trusted a man who drives a foreign car!' Having clearly passed a test, this was followed by brandy-laced tea and a three-hour lecture on the legacy of Roman viticulture in Britain: 'My young boy, the Romans grew vines in the first and second centuries in Lincolnshire, did you know?'

The major's own wine tasted like something better suited to cleaning Mozza's paintwork, but his enthusiasm was infectious. As I peered through his tall Georgian drawing room window, the rain splattering against it distorting what little light there was, he assured me that Kent enjoyed more sunshine hours than the south of France. I could just about see the waterlogged lawn stretching away into a grey infinity. Who was I to question the major's passionate assertions about Kent's Mediterranean climate?

Then there was a lady in Sussex who conducted our entire interview inside her greenhouse, sitting perched on a vast upturned terracotta pot like a rare exotic bird. She had soil-caked hands and spent most of the time extolling the virtues of her beloved peppers and tomatoes. The air was thick with the heady perfume of the ripening fruit and compost and her wine sat in recycled lemonade bottles and demijohns along one shelf. I wasn't sure whether it was fermenting or decomposing and she'd pause every so often to mist her precious peppers, creating rainbow halos with the spray. She poured me a generous tasting of her Müller-Thurgau wine, which looked as appealing as a wet weekend in Margate. It didn't taste that way at all though. It had more energy to it than 'The Big One' at Blackpool pleasure beach, all zippy acidity with clean, crisp gooseberries and quince. I think she might also have dropped a few of her tomatoes in the blend, though, as I definitely got a good whiff of those too.

A retired colonel in Kent, I discovered, thought he was a climate-change prophet. He'd planted his vines after the scorching summer of 1976, only to discover that climate change hadn't reached British shores *quite* yet – that year had merely been more a meteorological blip, a rare miracle of uninterrupted English sunshine. His leather-bound temperature records, like his tasting notes, were more 'hope' than accuracy.

It was here, on my third pilgrimage to Kent, that Mozza finally staged her revolt. The old girl had endured nearly a thousand miles, bouncing down rutted farm tracks and languishing in vineyard car parks and now she'd had enough. The crank handle, always reluctant but usually eventually cooperative, spun with fruitless enthusiasm. Each turn produced nothing but a clunk. The colonel, who'd been watching my increasingly desperate efforts, emerged as if he'd been waiting all afternoon for this opportunity, clutching a bottle of what he proudly announced as his 'limited release' sparkling Ortega, the label slightly wonky and clearly printed on his home printer.

He leant against the recalcitrant Mozza in the last patch of evening sunshine and performed an elaborate uncorking ceremony. The wine fizzed into our glasses with all the enthusiasm of a Monday-morning commuter. It had a few bubbles, many fewer than a Champagne, and its acidity could have unblocked Mozza's exhaust, but somehow none of that mattered. It had found its perfect moment. 'Hilariousness in a glass', it was like the colonel's dreams fermented and bottled, and I'm sure the world is a better place for it being a truly limited release.

We stood there, the colonel and I, waiting for the AA, watching swallows diving over his vines as he told stories of vintages past and his hopes for the future of English wine. By the time the AA van appeared, grinding up the gravel drive about two hours later, I'd learned volumes from the old colonel about wine, how it's grown and made. Filling time with unplanned chat, I'd discovered a drive and a passion that I've grown to realise is shared by all good winemakers; an unwavering belief that what they're actually creating is a story – as tasty a story as possible about their place, their vines and their people. This is something you can't comprehend by studying in a classroom or walking up the wine aisles in your local wine shop: you've got to get out and see these people and places to really understand it.

I researched my wine thesis less in libraries than through conversations with these enthusiastic eccentrics, and much of what I gleaned from them has come to pass. This is thrilling for the English and Welsh wine trade, less so in terms of the devastating consequences of global climate change – hardly something to celebrate over a flute of Kent fizz. But as our climate has grown warmer, England is now producing mind-blowingly good, award-winning sparkling wines. Proof is in the pudding with famous Champagne houses having bought land in southern England and starting production of sparkling wine there. Taittinger, for example, at Domaine Evremond in Kent; and Pommery with Louis Pommery in Hampshire. Indeed, I've marched alongside Stephen Duckett of Hundred Hills winery up a vine-covered chalk hillside in Oxfordshire which, he assures me, is pretty much the same geological make-up as the Côte de Blancs vineyards of Champagne. That land in Champagne sells, if and when it ever does, for over £1.5 million per hectare, while the best vineyard land in the UK goes for considerably less than £100,000 a hectare. So, it doesn't take Einstein to understand why Taittinger are sending their tentacles over the channel. No more Gallic shrugs from them, and there will surely be more French houses following.

Meanwhile, we're developing our own home-grown expertise here in the UK and we can all go and witness it. Our vineyards and wineries are gearing up brilliantly to tours, tastings and hospitality, a bit like Australia began some thirty years ago. My mind was recently blown visiting Dermot Sugrue in Sussex, a plucky Irishman with a fancy for racing bicycles and perhaps one of the UK's most talented winemakers. Dermot invited me to taste a bottle of his 'Trouble with Dreams', a wine he'd made ten years previously – it was like being hit with a 300-volt prod, a wine so full of energy, ripeness and green apple and citrus fruit, and it had developed that smell of a bakery at nine in the morning when all the croissants, pains au chocolat, cinnamon buns and the like, have just come out of the oven. I had no idea English sparkling wine could age so brilliantly and Dermot took the time to explain to me how it all came about. It is a charming and funny story, and I urge you to look it up – or even better, pay a visit to Dermot's vineyard for yourself.* You don't get that first-hand experience without getting out there and in amongst it and you don't need to be a wine professional to be welcomed either, you just need to have an interest.

In the last twenty to thirty years, I've witnessed the English wine industry really growing up. Today, we've swapped our charming tweed-clad dreamers for professionals with good financial backing and highly skilled vignerons and winemakers who, although they could work anywhere in the world, choose to stay in England for its challenge and potential. These are the new pioneers, armed with science and skill and the investment needed to make it all happen. Compared to France, we're currently a cottage industry, producing a modest 21 million or so bottles each year (Champagne alone churns out over 300 million bottles per annum). And yes, some of the prices might seem high. But consider the journey: from my old colonel's questionable sparkling Ortega to English sparkling wines that make the redoubtable houses of Champagne nervous. It's like watching the awkward teenager who played village cricket suddenly walking out to bat at Lord's.

In 1993, my dissertation complete, I graduated from Oxford Brookes University (née Oxford Polytechnic), eager to be part of this English wine revolution I believed I'd discovered. First, I researched oenology courses at Roseworthy in Adelaide and Davis in California, but realised that I fell very short in the chemistry department. I did find a suitable course, though, at the only winemaking school in England: Plumpton College, down near Brighton in East Sussex. To

---

* www.sugruesouthdowns.com/pages/tastings-events

pay for my fees, I went in search of a job . . . and I got one. It was anything but glamorous but it was to be another schooling in what wine was really all about.

No graduate training scheme at Majestic Wine Warehouse for me, I wanted to get in among the vines; to get my hands dirty with winemaking. But there was no romantic French château, no ancient cellar in Tuscany – only a collection of steel tanks in a converted barn in Twyford, Berkshire, three miles from Mum and Dad's. This was Thames Valley Vineyards where I spent the next year and a half, most of my time up to my elbows in abrasive cleaning fluid, chastising myself for my lunatic career choice, wishing I'd studied harder at school, and so grateful for my two days a week when I was released for my winemaking course at Plumpton.

My boss was John Worontschak, who was born to Ukrainian parents in Adelaide, Australia, where he'd worked for Petaluma, Penfolds and Yalumba, all wineries with huge reputations and credibility. But he'd travelled the world with wine, and had even worked at Hugel, one of the best wineries in Alsace – in fact, one of the best in all of France. John had landed in England in the mid-eighties, where he was, and is still today, a mover and shaker in his adopted country's wine world. This was a CV that made me dribble with respect and I looked up to him with awe and a bit of fear. He laughs about it now but, to tell the truth, I found him utterly terrifying, more than any teacher I'd ever had, perhaps because he was the only teacher I'd ever really wanted to impress.

In those days, John was what they called a 'flying winemaker'. He made wine for supermarkets, jetting between continents and coming back to base to praise us, sometimes, but help us always and liberally point out the things that needed doing. Flying winemakers were a thing of the early nineties and John was one the most respected internationally. He and a small number of others went all over the world, particularly areas with lots of vines and even more mediocrity, swooping into tired wineries to rescue them from obscurity.

These flying winemakers had new ideas that seem so simple and basic today – keep everything spotlessly clean, keep the temperature low during fermentation, and you'll be rewarded with a wine that has bright fruit and elegance, a practice that's now commonplace in every contemporary winery. They'd parachute into the Languedoc in the south of France, once considered one of the biggest toilets of wine production; and to Eastern Europe – Bulgaria, Romania and other areas with brilliant potential but having got nowhere close to realising it. With an insistence on gleaming stainless-steel tanks, they took the old-guard wineries by the scruff of the neck, gave them a good shake and transformed their substandard wines into acceptable.

And at Thames Valley Vineyards, that's what my job was. Keeping things clean and helping to create not just acceptability but excellence.

On my very first morning, I remember I strode up to the winery like I was going for a day out at Henley Royal Regatta – pristine beige chinos, a crisp blue button-down shirt, and a pair of brand-new deck shoes. John took one look at me and my garb and smiled a sort of knowing smile. He knew what I had in store – a long day wading through lakes of fermenting grape juice.

'So why are you here? What do you know about working in a winery?' he asked.

I stuttered for a bit, stammered for a bit more, then, once

he'd realised he couldn't persuade me differently, he introduced me to his number two, Vince Gower, and I got to work.

John and Vince were like chalk and cheese – like Petrus meets Kylie Minogue's Prosecco. Vince was tall and lean and moved through the winery with calm precision. John provided the excitement and the theoretical framework, usually in rapid-fire bursts between flights to South Africa or wherever some winery or other needed him next. With Vince, everything had its time and its place, then the tornado would sweep in tasting everything, scribbling instructions then vanishing again leaving us to implement his latest brainwave.

But it was Vince who taught me the job of winemaking. He was so absolutely unflappable. He could watch a tank of Schönburger (another weird and wonderful grape variety) burst its seams without so much as raising an eyebrow. He was the ideal foil to John, carrying out every task to his boss's exacting standards – no complaints, no compromise. He wore his expertise lightly and spotted any problems, which I definitely missed, maintaining the serene air of someone who'd clearly seen it all before and knew exactly what needed to be done. In those early weeks, I remember that I had attached a pump – or rather I'd 'sort of' attached it – to a fresh fermenting vat to see a river of white wine heading out of the winery and straight down a drain hole, and to Vince this fiasco seemed like just another Tuesday morning. He was methodical, disciplined, with a casual approach and an encyclopaedic knowledge. He knew every pipe, every valve and every filter. I must have driven him mad with my questions, but he humoured me, making even my most mundane tasks seem to me like they were making a vital impact on the process.

However, if you think winemaking is romantic, try

scrubbing the inside of a steel tank at seven on a February morning in a winery with no heating... of course.

'Clean tanks and clean pipes make clean wines,' Vince would say.

I heard this so many times I started muttering it in my sleep. Most of my days were spent cleaning. Every surface had to be spotless, every piece of equipment sanitised to within an inch of its life. I'd go home smelling of cleaning solution and have nightmares about my skin dissolving in a tub of caustic soda.

In those first few months under Vince's keen eye, I learned more about what *not* to do than I ever learned about what *to do*.

DO NOT #1: roll a barrel on its side – rather, keep it upright, and roll it on its bottom edge. You're not rolling a baguette!

DO NOT #2: put your head anywhere near the top of a fermenting tank, *ever* (unless you want to breathe in carbon dioxide, pass out, fall in and drown).

Yet, by watching, listening and working alongside Vince and John I learned so much more than I could ever have learned working in any wine shop – I was experiencing first-hand how wine was made. Between John's surprise inspections, Vince would explain things as we worked – *why* we were doing what we were doing, what could go wrong, and what should go right.

And then they'd do their tastings. I'd be on all fours in the winery's vat room trying to work out which end of the pump the wine was going to fly out of whilst peering through the glass window that looked into John's lab-cum-tasting room. I'd watch John explaining intricate flavours and aromas to

Vince and I'd crave to be in there too, learning how and why my list of winery tasks might materialise in the wines. Sometimes they'd invite me to their tasting sessions, and I'd try not to wet myself with nerves. Vince would have lined up glasses of everything we had made and together we would swirl, sniff, taste, spit. As if my opinion mattered at all. John's palate was unlike anything I had come across yet – he could taste nuances in the wine that I couldn't even pronounce.

'Getting some ethyl acetate here,' he'd opine, while I tried to remember if that was a good or a bad thing to taste in the wine (turns out it's a bad thing, like nail polish remover if you've got too much). But gradually I got the hang of this tasting lark. These were wines *before* they were wines, I now understood: unfinished, cloudy and unrefined. We had to look into these glasses of sludge and seek out anything that was missing or out of kilter. And I realised I was slowly, somehow, learning a bit about winemaking. Not enough to trust myself, but I was definitely learning. With every tank I cleaned, every pump I primed, every filter I changed and every sample I tasted, I got another little piece of the jigsaw. The glamorous stuff would come later, maybe, but this was where I acquired the fundamentals: cleanliness, attention to detail, analytical tasting – and the ability to roll with the punches when instructed to give this or that enormous tank yet another scrub.

I realise now how lucky I was to start out with those two, John and Vince. I also think I must have been a bit nuts to begin my apprenticeship in an English vineyard, and to decide to study oenology in a Sussex winemaking school having just scraped a low C in my Chemistry O level. John may have terrified me but then at just twenty-three, I was easily terrified.

His standards were rigorous and they needed to be – he was making wine that had to be consistent, clean, and able to survive being shipped across oceans to sit on supermarket shelves around the world. And Vince? Well, he taught me that good winemaking isn't just about the glamour and the knowledge – it's about the graft, the attention to detail, and yes, the endless, endless cleaning.

Today's wine world, where techniques and ideas flow freely across borders, owes much to the flying winemaker pioneers like John who lived out of suitcases and weren't afraid to tell the owners of centuries-old estates that they might want to consider scouring their tanks properly once in a while. They showed me that sometimes the best way to respect tradition is to know when to break it.

HOW TO TASTE WINE

These tips might sound a bit bossy, but bear with me. To really understand the flavours and nuances of wine it helps to follow some simple steps. It's all about the Six Ss for me and here's how I go about it:

1. SET everything up properly before you start. Make sure the wine for tasting is at the right temperature: for whites and rosés, 8–10°C; for reds, 12–18°C. Open the wine at least half an hour, or sometimes more, before you taste, white wines included. Then pour into a clean glass.

2. SEE what's in the glass. Take a good look, as this will give you the first signals. Does the wine look in good condition, with no haziness, for example? If it's a white wine, is it pale or rich in colour? Generally speaking, the richer the colour the richer the wine. If it's a red wine, how dark is it? A darker colour generally indicates a fuller-bodied wine.

3. SWIRL. Gently move the wine around the glass and it will start to release its lovely aromas. Now, check the wine's 'legs', or how the tears fall down the inside of the glass as you swirl. Are they moving quickly or are they thick and slow? The latter is an indication of a high-alcohol wine.

4. SNIFF. Hover your nose at the mouth of the glass and pay attention to your first sniff of the wine – that first smell will give you most aroma. Does it smell good? Is it fruity, indicating a young wine? Or are there other scents in the mix? A richness of honey, tobacco, leather, all sorts of smells, may suggest that the wine might have a bit of bottle age on it.

5. **SLURP.** Get a good measure of wine in your mouth and move it all around your tongue and palate. If you want to look and sound like a true pro, purse your lips and suck in a bit of air (taking care not to aspirate a lungful of vino). This is an oxygen injection for the wine in your mouth which helps open up the flavours so they reach all the important bits of your palate.

6. **SPIT** or **SWALLOW**? That is the question. For my work I have to spit. I am often tasting tens, sometimes up to a hundred wines in a day, and if I swallowed all of them I'd be struggling to make it standing to tea time. But beware, even if you spit, a little alcohol seeps into the bloodstream, so you will still get that warm fuzziness after tasting a few times. So leave the car keys behind.

Wine Wanker Approved List #2: Ten Favourite Aussie Wines

(**Hero bottle** – *Brokenwood Hunter Valley Semillon, New South Wales*)

Jim Barry 'Cover Drive' Cabernet Sauvignon, Clare Valley, South Australia

This wine reminds me of the Bulgarian Cabernet Sauvignon I used to buy in Sainsbury's in the early nineties . . . only it's way better. Although it's a touch more than my budget back then of £3.99, it's a style of wine I love for its ripeness, juiciness, and all-round full-bodied deliciousness. And it's still great value.

Grant Burge 'Filsell' Old Vine Shiraz, Barossa Valley, South Australia

In my early years, I loved full-bodied reds and this one stood out for me by quite some way. It's from a single vineyard in Barossa (Filsell, funnily enough) with very old vines and a team who've been making wine for a long, long time – they know what they're doing. It's a full-bodied, black, spicy bombshell of a Shiraz that I still love today.

Shiraz, Heartland Wines, Langhorne Creek, South Australia

This is a beauty from Aussie winemaker Ben Glaetzer at Heartland. A black and brooding, heady Shiraz – the sort that got me into New World wines as I first knew them. Today it's still a cracker and great value to boot.

Cabernet Sauvignon, Moss Wood, Margaret River, Western Australia
Every wine that Moss Wood release is a belter and this Cabernet Sauvignon is too delicious for words. It's brimming with black fruit and has the structure to age gracefully in bottle, so you can attack the first bottle with pleasure as soon as you've bought it and forget about the other(s) for quite some time.

Keyneton Estate Euphonium, Henschke Barossa Valley, South Australia
Henschke, one of Australia's oldest family-owned wineries, make some of the country's most expressive, most expensive, most sought-after wines, but this Shiraz blend is my favourite. My 'go to' for the price. It's classy and classic with all the black pepper spice I seek in a big, bold Aussie red.

Petaluma Chardonnay, Piccadilly Valley, South Australia
When I first tasted this, I knew I was working for the right man – John Worontschak who'd made wine at this vineyard in the Adelaide Hills, South Australia. It's a knock-out Aussie Chard with incredible balance and elegance.

The Steading Shiraz, Torbreck Vintners, Barossa Valley, South Australia
If Moss Wood's my favourite Aussie Cabernet, then Torbreck are right up there for the Shiraz prize. A very different style from the Henschke I mentioned earlier, I love this wine for its muscle and rusticity. For me, it's playing much more of a Northern Rhône game.

Dry Red No. 1, Yarra Yering, Yarra Valley, Victoria
I came across this wine hiding in the corner of an Oxford college cellar when I was trying to sell twenty dozen bottles of Pinot Grigio to a catering manager. He opened the bottle, poured me a glass, and it blew my socks off. It's a Cabernet-Sauvignon-based wine so loads of blackcurrant but with an extra hint of mint, which is totally sensational.

Wynns Coonawarra Estate 'Black Label' Cabernet Sauvignon, Coonawarra, South Australia
Coonawarra does special things to Cabernet Sauvignon. It's all about the soil type here – Terra Rossa, which is rich in iron and gives the good wines here an intensity and vitality that I love. Here's a great example.

Yabby Lake Pinot Noir, Mornington Peninsula, Victoria
Yabby Lake make wines with extraordinary energy and vibrancy. This is a light, fresh and juicy red with crunchy red fruit and wonderful texture. It's flying the flag for Aussie Pinot.

3
First Love

DOMAINE TESTUT
Chablis
APPELLATION CHABLIS CONTRÔLÉE

Vieilles Vignes

1990

Hero bottle: *Chablis, Domaine Testut, Burgundy*

In the world of wine, terroir is mother nature showing us what she, along with her changing seasons' elements, can do with a vine and a patch of earth – that holy trinity of grape, soil and climate working together to produce something truly unique. The region of Burgundy, in central eastern France, stands as terroir's spiritual capital, a tapestry of vineyards where a distance of just ten paces can mean the difference between mediocrity and greatness.

A little bit of history. About two million years ago, Burgundy was covered by sea; this formed the area's limestone and marl (limestone-clay mix) soils, and it is this that gives Burgundian wines their characteristic and much-coveted mineral tang. The wine history in Burgundy is long; some believe that the Celts may have been producing wine here before the Romans colonised Gaul, in 51 BC. The Romans brought with them an ancient knowledge of viticulture, establishing vineyards across the region's fertile, mineral-rich slopes. After the fall of the Roman Empire, the Catholic church and the monks took ownership of much of the Burgundy land and so assumed the winemaking duties. Cistercian monks spent tens of centuries here, mapping every subtle variation in soil and slope.

Here in Burgundy, wine speaks of place more eloquently

than anywhere else on earth. This is one of France's most famous wine-growing regions, and at its northernmost frontier sits the small village of Chablis, like a watchful sentinel, where Chardonnay finds its purest voice among those ancient seabeds turned to limestone and clay. Here, where this green-skinned white-wine grape is vulnerable to extreme weather and spring frosts, you'll find it speaking in whispers of minerals and rain-washed stones rather than shouting with oak and tropical fruit.

I fell for Chablis early – only a little while before I fell for my wife Beth. In the Eton Wine Bar it was a best-selling white wine and one which both Dad and Uncle Mick adored. Whenever any customers left a bottle with a dribble in the bottom, I'd be on it like a rat up a drain pipe, sprinting over to clear their table and pour the rest into a glass.

Chablis was also pretty key in marking a moment in time and place that was to change my life entirely and forever . . . The spot was a little French bistro in Great Clarendon Street in Jericho, Oxford. And the time was mid-February in 1992, Valentine's night to be precise. This was an early date with Beth, my long-suffering wife of nearly thirty years, and with a bottle of 1990 Chablis by Domaine Testut.

Not to boast, but all in all, as a Valentine's date, it was pretty damn perfect. I could not have chosen a more romantic spot, like something straight out of a Richard Curtis film, in fact – all misty Victorian lampposts, flickering lights and a street lined with beautiful old Grade 2 listed stone buildings. There I was, nineteen years old, walking Beth to one of the city's best restaurants. I'd never been there before but Dad knew it and assured me that I was onto a winner.

Inside it oozed grown-up charm. Wall-to-wall couples,

all seeming to know exactly which fork to use first, and all smart professional or academic looking – professors, doctors, authors, maybe, all with their perfect posture. And there was me, feeling about as comfortable as a vegan in the butcher's, trying not to set my napkin on fire with the table candle.

Beth, however, just twenty years old, her chestnut hair catching the candlelight like a Pinot Noir in finest cut crystal, seemed to be taking it in her stride. There she was, 5'6" of pure sparkle, with a smile to turn the dreariest day of the week into a Friday night. She just radiated kindness and mischief, all wrapped up in a seemingly effortless class. A bit like a cracking glass of Chablis, in fact. I was in safe hands.

A waiter pottered over. 'Would sir like to see the wine list?'

Of course, sir would like to see the wine list. He'd never been asked before, but yes, indeedy, sir could definitely do with a drink and he was sure his date could too.

He disappeared briefly, then back he came with what to me looked like the complete works of Shakespeare bound up between two sheets of worn brown leather. It was probably just a perfectly standard restaurant wine list, but then I was used to Uncle Mick's carefully curated, simple single page, so working out which way up to hold this tome – let alone where to start and what to order from it – was daunting, to say the least.

Timidly, as I leafed through the pages trying my hardest to look as if I knew what I was doing, I asked Beth whether she'd like red or white. 'White,' she replied, quickly and confidently as I hurriedly thumbed through the other half of the pages. And there it was, just as she said, the heading: 'White Wines'. I had hit the Burgundy section and there, at the top of the left-hand page, was listed a bottle of Domaine Testut Chablis 1990, exactly the same bottle of wine that Uncle Mick served in the wine bar, except here it cost £5 more than they sold it for. A moment of pure relief – like spotting a friend at a party full of strangers. Never had the name of a wine looked so welcome, or a decision been made quite so quickly.

Thank goodness for familiar wine! My security blanket in times of need.

And then along came the waiter, our bottle in hand, its label as I remembered it and oozing an aura of *You've got this, Tom!*

He presented it to me; I nodded as authoritatively as I could and he poured the taste into my glass. I'd done this many times for customers at the wine bar, so I knew his drill – I just didn't know mine. Instinctively, though, I said, 'Thank you. I'm sure it's fine!'

Allow me a bit of a moan here (there'll be more when you get to the bit about sommeliers) but it drives me mad when waiters pour a bog-standard wine to taste at the table. Unless it's to check whether I actually like the wine, which I don't think it is (it's really for us to check if the wine is in good condition), it seems about as helpful as the car mechanic inviting me to look under the bonnet after they've serviced my car . . . just to check it looks OK.

Anyway, back to the date. The waiter poured a large glass for Beth then topped mine up, too. It was delicious. More relief! My date and I cheersed, my shoulders relaxed and I took a very large gulp . . .

Holy cow, that Chablis was good. Something else, in fact. It warmed me from the inside out . . . and quickly. It was bright with green apples, cool with mineral, stony notes and, unlike me that evening, elegant. It made me forget that I was trying to impress and allowed me to be . . . well, just me. Beth clearly saw how excited I was, and she heard it too, as I couldn't stop gabbling at her that this was the Chablis that Dad and Uncle Mick imported . . . one of my favourite wines on their list . . . and on I gibbered.

'It's like clean sheets,' Beth cut in. 'All fresh and flowery.' With the state of our student house and my room at the time, I could only take her word for it.

Around us, couples were getting very Valentinesy. All hushed voices, lots of gazing into eyes and holding of hands. But at our table, I think, something different was unfolding. The wine was doing its thing, not just in my glass but in the space between us. Beth got the giggles, her confidence growing, which made mine grow too. I began to worry less about being the freshers in the restaurant and instead joined Beth in her favourite sport – listening in to the people on the next-door table and bringing as much gossip and slander back to our conversation as possible.

The food lived up to everything Dad had promised. Plump scallops resting on their shells like jewels nestled in pools of herb-flecked melted butter. With the flinty, fresh Chablis – bliss. My main course was lamb, I remember, pink as a sunset with a perfect herb crust and a red wine sauce that had clearly been reducing since breakfast. By then I couldn't have cared if the Chablis went with the lamb. Both were delicious and Beth had me doubled up with laughter pointing out that the woman two tables away had her shoes on the wrong way round.

We had fun that night and, as outside the street grew

quieter, our bottle of Chablis became less my prop and more our companion for the evening. Like all good wingmen, it knew when to take a back seat and let the real magic happen. When, finally, we stepped out into the dark Oxford night, I clutched the empty bottle in one hand. And when Beth put her small warm hand in the other, my head nearly blew clean off. Even now, more than thirty years later, that dizzy feeling hasn't quite gone away.

I didn't know it at the time, but that bottle, that label, marked the start of our life together; a first chapter, a lucky romantic charm hiding behind apparent simplicity, it had depth and it revealed it over time – a bit like Beth herself, really. None of this I was registering at the time, mind you. I was just a slightly inept boy trying not to screw up a big date, and it must have worked.

Back at my house, I carefully soaked the label off the bottle and stuck it safely in my wine-label book. Next to it, I just wrote: 'Date with Beth Martin'. (Oh, to see nineteen-year-old Tom's face if I could go back in time and tell him, 'Well, guess what? Four years from now, you marry her!')

I guess I was lucky then. Lucky enough to have had some wine experience through Dad, Uncle Mick and working at the wine bar, and very lucky that I'd quickly spotted a wine I recognised in that giant leather-bound volume. Had I not, I'd have either gone straight for the house wine or succumbed to a panic attack. It still happens to me today. If I have to flick through a wine list for more than five minutes, I get flustered and agitated which, thirty years ago, would have manifested itself as fear and a sickly sweat on my brow.

For me, then and now, wine is about the moment, rather than the moment being about the wine. I don't believe any

FIRST LOVE

good moment is ever about the wine. At meals, I think the food should lead and the wine should follow. The wine simply serves to enhance both the good moments and the food. Neither, in terms of pairing, does it necessarily have to be the perfect match as declared by the sommeliers and wine writers – if the wine is good and the meal is good, the company good too, the celebration is already right there. And the wine will be remembered, at least by me, for the part it played in that mix.

Chablis, both its wine and its landscape, has marked my life in wine in such a profound way. It was actually in Chablis, ten years later, that I really got to understand and taste terroir. I was accompanying my boss at the time, Jack Scott, on his annual pilgrimage to visit his regular wine growers in France. A memorable trip, let's just say, that could have been scripted by P.G. Wodehouse.

Jack Scott is the kind of Englishman the French secretly wish they'd invented. More English than a cucumber sandwich, if he could have mounted a figurine of Admiral Nelson to the bonnet of his car he'd have absolutely done so, and for this trip, we were travelling in his mum's green Bentley.

'They'll love it,' he declared with complete conviction. 'The French only make crap cars, so they'll love a glorious bit of Britishness rolling up to their gates. You wait and see.'

And they did. They adored him and they marvelled at her, the green Bentley. As did they marvel at his imagined mastery of their language. He spoke French with the kind of gusto that made accuracy secondary to entertainment, yet he somehow managed to charm every vigneron from Champagne to the Rhône. Here was an Englishman who appreciated French traditions as much as his own, he understood their wines as he did British cars, and could match them story for story over a five-hour lunch . . . and he didn't even drink.

Travelling in the Bentley was like being transported in a drawing room on wheels, complete with burled walnut picnic tables and more leather than a gentlemen's club reading room. While the suspension on normal cars absorbs bumps and potholes, the Bentley seemed to just . . . shoo them away. As such, we didn't so much drive through French countryside, as waft across it, floating over roads like the Bentley was a grand stately home off on holiday. Instead of a roar, she purred, like a smug snooty cat. A nudge of the steering wheel from Jack, she would consider thoughtfully before she elegantly complied, and speed was achieved on the Bentley's terms, too – not through acceleration, as such, rather seemingly through a genteel gathering of momentum, as if she were merely adjusting our schedule to arrive at the next lunch on time.

By the time we reached our first stop, in Champagne, I was comfortably settled into this new mode of transport. We were eccentrics on tour, greeted there by Jack's wine-growing friends with a bottle of Premier Cru Champagne and epic quantities of perfectly cooked *côte de boeuf*. But next Chablis awaited us and with it, a revelation.

Just after nine on that spring morning in 2002, as we approached Chablis from the north on the *route départementale* D91, the first vines came into view, shrouded in morning mist. But then, as we crested the next hill, nature decided to put on a show. Before us this huge glacial valley opened up like a curtain lifting to reveal an amphitheatre bathed in rich, golden light. The temperature rose noticeably – I could feel the warmth through my passenger-side window – and suddenly the mighty Grand Cru vineyards of Chablis stretched out before us, their vines climbing up the hill towards greatness in perfect formation. These high Grand Cru slopes, I learned, bask in up to three hours more sunlight than their less fortunate cousins – so it's no wonder their vines produce wines with more richness and complexity than the Petit Chablis I'd been treating myself to when payday allowed. And, seeing the terroir with my own eyes, it was so, so simple to understand.

We rolled through the sleepy town with the morning finding its feet, past weatherworn limestone buildings, down narrow streets where the green Bentley almost had to breathe in. As we approached the Café de la Poste in the centre, breakfasting workers rose to give us a standing ovation – mid-croissant, coffee cups in hand. Jack acknowledged them with a royal wave as we wafted on slowly towards Domaine de la Meulière. Our route wound through the vineyards, the Bentley's flying spur pointing the way to our next great wine discovery.

As we crunched up the gravel drive of the domaine, Monsieur and Madame Laroche circled the car like children around a Christmas tree, exclaiming, '*Ooo la laaa, mon dieu*, my god!'

'They'll spend the first half hour stroking it and jumping in and out of the driver's seat. You watch,' Jack had predicted that morning. And that's exactly what they did, with an enthusiasm that made me wonder if we were at a wine tasting or had taken a wrong turn into a vintage car sale.

In the Laroche's tasting room, though, everything changed. In front of us was a full range of wines, representing all the different vineyards they made wine from, all Chardonnay but all different. And behind them stood our hosts, like artists exhibiting their latest works. Madame Laroche scuttled off to refill the tray of Gruyère *gougères*, cheesy choux pastry puffs that were as moreish as a box of chocolates. And I'd know – I scoffed most of them in just two mouthfuls. Then Monsieur Laroche started pulling out rare old bottles from left, right and centre as if producing them out of a hat, pointing with his grubby fingers at various points of the vineyard map to let us know which plot each particular wine came from. Jack was right. We'd shown up in the Bentley and now the Laroches were treating us to bottles it seemed even they'd forgotten they had stashed away. The imperious old English car changed the game.

It was two particular bottles of their 2000 Premier Crus, though, a 'Vaucoupin' and a 'Mont de Milieu', that gave me my terroir fix. Same vintage, same winemaking, same everything – except for the little patch of dirt the different vines called home. The Vaucoupin tasted austere, like I was actually licking a fossil, while the Mont de Milieu was an expansive powerhouse, all citrus oils and honey, with a hint of marzipan. The terroir penny didn't just drop for me then, it plummeted.

I had to get out and see where this Mont de Milieu vineyard actually was. I was beyond excited and it wasn't just the effects of the wine. Vincent, their son, could see this and offered to take us on a tour of the Laroche vineyards. Outside, I was like a toddler at the beach, kicking at rocks and collecting marine fossils as we walked – oyster shells, ammonites and nautiluses – literal pieces of 150-million-year-old Jurassic history that I could pick up and hold in my hand.

One particularly fine specimen made its way back to London, smuggled in my jacket pocket. It still sits on my desk today as a little reminder of why I get up in the mornings.

Before Jack and I knew it, the two hours we'd scheduled that morning for our visit to Domaine Laroche had turned into five, complete with a *dejeuner simple* after our vineyard tour: a platter of *pâté de campagne* and unctuous *L'Affiné au Chablis*, the local cow's milk cheese, with mountains of fresh crusty bread, and to finish, a simple pear tart to send us to sleep. We'd need to have another look at our schedule for the week if this was how we were to roll.

For keen winos like me, Chablis, and the whole of Burgundy for that matter, is a region that screams TERROIR from the hilltops – this magical French concept that was practically my third word after 'Mummy' and 'Daddy', and one that's kept me on the sauce ever since. If you don't get the gist of terroir from a tasting here on the ground in Chablis, well, you've got the wrong person helping you find it.

Chablis, too, is a reference point for many restaurant wine lists. It's a classic wine that serves as an anchor for the rest of the white wines on any wannabe-serious wine list. It adds gravitas and quality, and allows the other whites to dance round it with confidence. For me, it's like an anchor, a safe pick, because it's usually really blinking good.

Since serving Domaine Testut in the Eton Wine Bar and drinking that same wine on my date with Beth in 1992, Chablis got the memo about inflation. I've watched its steady march up the pricing ladder from £25 or so back then, to now, thirty-three years later, knocking on the door of £70. Yet while the price tags have grown more serious the wine itself remains unchanged. Humble in fact. Neither showy nor shouty, just that same brilliant expression of sense of place and that cool-climate precision, each bottle capturing a moment in time. Chablis, like most great wines, is made from one year's harvest, from one specific patch of vines, by people who care more about their land than their bank balance. Unlike mass-produced wines that aim for consistency at all costs, these are wines that change and evolve, sometimes majestically, sometimes disastrously, but always fascinatingly.

Throughout France, in its best wine regions, Chablis included, the wine is strictly produced and classified according to a set of rules known as the *Appellation d'Origine Controlée* (AOC). The AOC is like a sacred covenant between vigneron and vine and tightly controlled to ensure the wines of each region maintain their tradition and identity. No artificial irrigation being a key requirement. That is until there is a real drought crisis when an individual AOC might intervene and allow a small amount of irrigation in order to spare the vines. Some might read this as the French just being stubborn but many, including me, absolutely love and admire this typical Gallic steadfastness. It sounds nuts but the French have a profound understanding that wine greatness comes from a vine that has had to work hard. Like most of us the week before pay day, vines denied easy access to water must dig deep to survive, throwing their roots deep down in search of moisture, sometimes through layers of history sometimes ten-plus metres deep.

It's hard to witness traditional French vignerons during a drought. They continually track the weather, in the knowledge that stress may lead to greatness, but it can also bring catastrophe. But it's this struggle that makes these traditional wines unique. It helps to explain why Chablis tastes the way it does – that green-apple fruit but with an intense minerality and a saline note you'll find nowhere else on earth, like it's almost been filtered through river stones and fossilised shells, with an acidity that cuts through like a winter's morning frost. In fact, it's all about fossils here. The earth is literally packed with them and they give Chablis its distinctive character. The best of these wines achieve a kind of tension between richness and restraint, making you think about geology and history, about the millions of years it took to create this particular soil, and the centuries of human 'know how' it took to realise that this was where Chardonnay could achieve something approaching perfection. But each bottle tells its own story – from the clear, crisp, tart-fruit freshness of Petit Chablis to the rich, honeyed complexity of the Grand Crus from the slopes facing the town like a natural amphitheatre – as the vines converse with the soil, year after year, decade after decade, their roots delving that little bit deeper with every passing year.

This is why 'real' wine – not necessarily expensive wine, but wine made with respect for terroir – can never be as consistent as your Starbucks or McDonald's. The whole point is that each year and each vineyard is different. It's almost going out of its way to be confusing and unreliable, but that is precisely the magic. While the big brands chase uniformity, the true vignerons of Chablis embrace their role as custodians of the land, translating as truthfully as possible what the vine and its subsoil deem to yield each year.

For me, the best Chablis is a wine to enjoy thoughtfully – mindfully, even. To drink it is to enter a millennia-old conversation between human and place. It is to understand that the finest Chablis vineyards face south-east, catching the morning sun while being protected from the harshest afternoon heat. And it's to truly appreciate why generations of winemakers have chosen to simply allow this particular patch of earth to speak through their wines, rather than imposing their own will upon it.

And that's the case with so many great wines. Talk to any passionate winegrower anywhere in the world and they'll tell you it's about so much more than just the grape. They'll tell you about the elements of nature that produce those flavours and textures. And when a winegrower does this well, it's enchanting. Some growers have told the story of their wine to me in the most extraordinarily brilliant yet simple terms, allowing me to really understand this most complex drink on earth. And on one memorable occasion, not only did I experience exactly this, but so did Beth along with twenty-two of our closest friends. It was in autumn 2006, when, to celebrate our tenth wedding anniversary which we'd just had that July, our great friends Gavin and Angela Quinney hosted us all at their beautiful nineteenth-century Château Bauduc, just south of Saint-Émilion near Bordeaux.

I'd figured that after ten years of being married to me, Beth deserved more than just dinner and drinks at the local – she deserved magic. And magic, as we already knew from previous holidays with our children, is Château Bauduc. It's on the edge of Créon a small market town bustling with colour and life. As you drive out into the countryside, through an unremarkable housing development, there is the entrance to the estate, two ancient stone pillars, beyond which stretches a vine-bordered drive, like a dream about the perfect French landscape. It was a dream that Gavin and Angela had, in fact, and in 1999, they'd followed their dream, sold up in the UK and moved lock, stock and barrel to the château and French-winemaking nirvana. Now here they were surrounded by 200 acres of beauty, bringing up their four children and building a life I still marvel at.

Our friends arrived on the Friday, a day after Beth and me, wide-eyed, most of them having never seen a French wine château before. The limestone walls glowed honey-gold in the late afternoon sun, and we could smell autumn in the air – our nostrils full of warm earth, dying leaves, and the sweet mustiness of nearly-fermented grapes.

At about 5 p.m., Gavin kicked off our anniversary weekend with his 'Château Bauduc Bonjour Tour', all of us with glasses of the Quinneys' own cold, fresh white wine in hand, of course. As Gavin led us through the vineyards, telling the story of the château and the land, as much with his hands as with words, he'd stop mid-row, pluck a rogue Sauvignon Blanc grape that had escaped the harvest, and explain the wine in our glasses to us in a way that made us all take another delicious gulp. Before long, it was as if we had all fallen under a spell – such was the magic of this place.

Little excites me more than seeing first-timers set foot in a winery, especially when they are guided by someone who really knows that they're doing. It always reminds me of my own early experiences in Beaujolais, Chablis, the Thames Valley Vineyards, and beyond – that feeling of sheer wonder. As Gavin explained the dance between nature and nurture, tradition and technology, everyone – even the very few (two I think) among us who really didn't give a hoot about wine or where it came from – fell into a bit of a trance. Gavin is hugely knowledgeable but, like all good wine communicators, he talks about his subject with so much humour and passion, along with a big smack of self-deprecation. He makes it interesting and fun, not just for a wine geek like me. Which, basically, just makes me love and admire him even more.

But it is the main anniversary celebration dinner on the Saturday evening that I really want to tell you about. We were going to Saint-Émilion, a medieval jewel in the heart of the most famous wine region in the world. It is one of the most beautiful places I have ever visited and one that you *must* have on your hit list. Built on (and of) a luminous limestone hillside, its narrow cobblestone streets wind their way up and down steep inclines, each turn revealing a postcard-worthy view that attracts tourists in their thousands. Thousand-year-old red-roofed mansions and merchants' houses with shuttered windows and geranium-filled flower boxes stand shoulder to shoulder along the lanes, gnarled grape vines peek over old weathered stone garden walls, and dark, cool wine cellars burrow deep beneath the streets. In the golden evening light, the town's pale limestone walls glowed rich amber, casting long shadows across the medieval square at the top.

Our destination was the Logis de la Cadène, one of the town's oldest and most classic restaurants, perfectly positioned on one of its steepest slopes which, with their slippery limestone cobbles, are best tackled in flat shoes, so off came any high heels.

Once inside the Logis de la Cadène, we felt like we'd stepped into a temple devoted to food, wine and festivities. Gavin had persuaded the chef to create a menu to make his chosen wine sing – Château La Tour Figeac 1996, a Grand Cru Classé from Saint-Émilion, so very decent indeed. 1996 – the year that Beth and I were married . . . of course Gavin had thought of that!

That night's meal was a riot of overindulgence and extreme Frenchness. The first course? Foie gras with caramelised figs and a scatter of sea salt. To start, Gavin had selected a special wine from his château. Bordeaux champions the Sémillon grape for its white wines, both dry and sweet, and Gavin's 'Trois Hectares', a dry, textural white, was made largely from ancient vines growing on the best plot on his land and fermented in new French oak barrels – the perfect accompaniment to the rich, fatty goose liver.

However, what came next *really* blew my pants off. Gavin was serving the red wine from magnums (twice the size of a normal wine bottle and as we soon found out, twice the fun). He'd double decanted it three hours beforehand – that's pouring it out into a jug, carefully discarding any sediment, then gently pouring it back into each magnum to allow the wine to breathe and settle – and it had worked a treat. He poured our La Tour Figeac a moment or two before the main course arrived. At our table of twenty-four, many of our friends knew little or nothing about wine and most had never been taught how to taste wine before. Gavin guided us through the process in as engaging and simple a way as he'd done during his Château Bauduc Bonjour Tour the evening before, urging us to pick up the subtle tobacco notes, the ripe, plum-like fruit character, and suggesting how the wine might work with the huge plates of *côte de boeuf* cooked *à point*, which the waiters were now placing on our table. *À point* is translated as 'medium-rare' but I think the French work to a different scale – it was definitely on the rarest side of medium-rare, but melt-in-your-mouth divine. Next came mountains of sides but, frankly, I was transfixed by the wine in my glass.

'You know that warm comforting smell you get when you open a really old chest of drawers?' Gavin asked us. 'That hint of aged, sun-warmed cedar, faded lavender sachets and the old wallpaper lining the bottom of the drawer? Do you get that in this wine?'

And there it was. We all 'got it'. It's exactly what this wine offered and suddenly, thanks to Gavin's prompt, we were all drinking our own little bit of personal history.

As I took my next sip, it was as if I'd been fumbling in the dark in a museum and someone had suddenly turned the light on to reveal a masterpiece by Caravaggio. The fruit notes deepened, the tannins softened, the tobacco became more pronounced, creating a harmony that had me, and us all, Gavin included, shaking our heads in wonder. This, I thought, really *was* magic.

That night in Saint-Émilion was another of those unforgettable wine and food revelations. Of course, the experience was heightened by the setting and the occasion, but also by Gavin's enthusiasm, which helped us to really appreciate the wonder, there in our wine glasses. This was one of those times when you take a mouthful of wine, and it makes one plus one equal three. This La Tour Figeac alone was superb, but with the beef, well, it became something else entirely – as if they were having a conversation, and allowing us to eavesdrop.

FIRST LOVE

HOW TO TALK 'WINE' (WITHOUT SOUNDING NAFF)

How to talk about wine, to communicate what you're tasting and how it's making you feel in a way that others might understand is perhaps the thing I find hardest and most maddening about our trade. But in Gavin I have met the greatest wine communicator I know – only using straightforward and unpretentious terms to describe what he's tasting so his audience know exactly what he's on about. So different to many others I've met in the trade who seem intent on using ten pretentious adjectives in every sentence without actually saying anything useful. 'This wine shows notes of crushed autumn leaves gathered by Victorian orphans on a Tuesday, with hints of unicorn tears and a finish that reminds one of reading Proust in the rain.' Well, that tells us precisely the square root of bugger all.

I get it, though. It's hard. But I've learned a huge amount by listening to how cooks and chefs talk about wine. I've worked with many great chefs in my time, and sometimes they're one-man bands, sometimes they're the heads of the brigade, and with very few exceptions, particularly when they're young, initially they're all nervous of wine and wine tastings. But, without a doubt, they're the most interesting people to drink and taste wine with. If I want my tasting note written in a way that I know people will understand and will immediately make me and everyone else want to drink the whole bottle, I'll get a chef to write it. Give them a glass of something, and often they go all quiet and timid, smelling nervously (which is extraordinary given their fierce reputation), but then they taste enthusiastically, look up at the ceiling and given the right prompting (and a few more sips), in their mind's eye, see their whole fridge, spice cupboard, fruit bowl and herb garden laid out in front of them. From the encyclopaedic flavour glossary in their heads, they will often conjure the names of flavours, spices and condiments we all know and understand (but which would never cross our minds when thinking about the taste of a wine) – cinnamon, star anise, cloves, nutmeg and more. Cooking smells – cooking bacon, fried onions, fresh bread, burnt toast. And also textures we can all relate to – oily, crunchy, unctuous. And there and then, without overthinking it, the chef will have given me a tasting note that makes me smile and makes me want to drink the wine – no self-consciousness, no pomposity, just dreamy, delicious descriptors that are both confoundingly original and unnervingly accurate.

So, with this in mind, here is my quick guide to describing what you taste.

1. **START WITH THE COLOUR** – red, greenish, yellow, pink, maybe orange. And remember, although we talk about white wine, it's never actually white. Be as precise as you can to elaborate on the shade you see in your glass, and, importantly, what you like or dislike about it. And compare it with something relatable . . . it looks like watery Ribena or a urine sample in a hospital.

2. **THINK ABOUT THE INTENSITY** of the wine colour. Stick to language you understand, and explain what the intensity means to you. How thick is it? Deep, rich colours, for example, generally tell you that the wine is full-bodied and punchy, and vice versa. Look for 'tears' or 'legs' too.

These are the drops that fall down the inside of the glass after a brief swirl. Thick, slow tears suggest a wine with high alcohol (and/or sugar) content which in turn means it's going to be full-bodied and rich.

3. SMELL IT. Swirl it around the glass gently first then describe the smell. Is it fruity? If so, what fruits does it remind you of? What else do you smell? Does it make you think of any vegetables, household or cooking smells? Only describe things that you actually smell in the glass, not ones you imagine you'd like to smell. And again, do you like the aroma? Does it make you feel happy? Uplifted?

4. NOW THE FUN PART. TASTE IT – take a good sip and swish it all around in your mouth. How intense is the taste? A powerful wine is a full-bodied wine, and one that will generally go well with food. Is it zingy, sharp and acidic? Or sweet, mellow and more dreamy?

5. MOST IMPORTANTLY, describe what you like about the wine, if you like it. What words will help others to think they might enjoy it too? If I don't really enjoy a wine, I won't usually bother talking about it or writing up any notes on it – there are too many other good wines waiting for me. But if someone I respect has recommended a wine to me, I'll have another taste and try to find what they like about it – if I still don't get it, it's time to move on. Quality wine is only quality wine if it tastes quality to you.

6. FINALLY, I like to talk about wine the way normal humans talk about things they love – it's not about showing off how many fancy wine terms I know. The point is to share

something I love with someone else in a way that makes them want to love it too. Sometimes for me a wine tastes like summer holidays in France. Sometimes, let's be honest, it tastes like someone liquefied their garden shed. There is no right or wrong, just go for it.

Wine Wanker Approved List #3: Ten Favourite French Classics

(**Hero bottle** – *Chablis, Domaine Testut, Burgundy*)

Muscadet Sèvre et Maine sur Lie, Gadais Père et Fils, Loire
Muscadet gets a bad rep and I'm usually the first to agree; much of it used to taste like battery acid. In the right hands, though, it's a magical wine – so crisp, often saline, carrying fresh acidity and bags full of green apple fruit – a match made in heaven with oysters and oily fish. Look out for a good grower like Domaine Gadais, drink it within two years maximum and serve it well chilled.

Le Passage Saint-Joseph, Domaine Stéphane Ogier, Côte-Rôtie, Northern Rhône
Syrah doesn't get purer than in the appellation of Saint-Joseph in the Northern Rhône and, in the hands of these masters, it's all black pepper and liquorice. Totally stunning.

Vouvray, Domaine Boutet Saulnier, Loire
If it's possible for wine to contain electricity then this wine definitely has it. It's so brilliantly bright, dry and fruity with an almost razor-like acidity, in a good way. It's like a whole English orchard – the pears, apples and quinces – all rammed into the bottle.

Sancerre, Gitton Père et Fils, Eastern Loire
When I first tasted this wine it took Sancerre to a completely new level for me. Today, Pascal Gitton's daughter Chanel has

joined him in the winemaking and their wines are even more sensational. For something truly special, splash out on a bottle of their oak-aged Les Herses Sancerre and strap yourself in before you unplug it.

Menetou-Salon 'Morogues', Domaine Henri Pellé, Loire
This is another Loire Sauvignon Blanc and a really good one at that. The vineyards of Menetou are just a bit further away from the river itself than Sancerre and Pouilly-Fumé. Here, Henri Pellé is the king, making magnificently fresh, energetic and characterful wines – all gooseberries, green apple and cut grass.

Chablis Premier Cru 'Les Vaillons', Domaine Samuel Billaud, Chablis
Samuel Billaud makes exceptional wine – even his least expensive Bourgogne Chardonnay is knock-out delicious, but if you stretch to one of his Premier Cru Chablis you'll be in for a real treat. This is the best Chablis I have ever tasted.

Bourgogne Rouge, Domaine Coche-Dury, Burgundy
I first tasted this in the cellar at Saint John's College in Oxford. It's the *'ordinary'* wine from the vineyards of the *'extraordinary'* Coche-Dury family, one of the most legendary growers in Burgundy, famed for white wines – eye-wateringly expensive ones at that – but this Pinot Noir was like having someone pour a bucket of strawberry jam over me.

Pernand-Vergelesses Premier Cru 'Les Vergelesses', Domaine Jean-Jacques Girard, Burgundy
If you like red Burgundy, you'll love this Pinot Noir from Pernand – bags of red fruit and mouth-filling spicy oak. It's a

belter every year I've tried it. Pernand-Vergelesses is right by the hill of Corton – incredible terroir and the wine is pretty hard to come by. If you see it, or any wine made by Jean-Jacques Girard for that matter, buy it – and especially this underrated and underpriced Pinot Noir. It's just delicious.

Classic Riesling, Domaine Hugel, Alsace
There are a few dynamite winegrowers in Alsace and their wines are still underpriced and undervalued. When I first tasted Hugel's Riesling, I was transported to a completely new world of white wine. Once you've discovered really tasty, dry Riesling, there's no turning back. And Hugel's a great place to start.

Pouilly-Fumé, Château de Tracy, Loire
The Pouilly-Fumé appellation lies across the Loire river from Sancerre, and while the wines here are also made from Sauvignon Blanc grapes, as the name suggests, Pouilly-Fumé adds a hint of fumé . . . smoke – think the head of a burnt match or the barrel of a gun. Sounds a bit bizarre, I know, but this wine is a cracker. Jack introduced me to this wine and it's when I first really 'got it', that smoky note.

4
F**k France

Hero bottle: *Cloudy Bay Sauvignon Blanc, Marlborough, New Zealand*

If you haven't got it yet, I confess, France, and its food, its wine and its people, have held a special place in my heart. It was in France that Beth and I celebrated our tenth wedding anniversary, and where we have spent many a holiday with our children. I just love it there, and always have done.

France has also been the foundation of every study on wine I have done. It still is for anybody looking to learn about wine via an accredited route such as the Wine & Spirit Education Trust, the key qualification, really, for anybody who wants to gain comprehensive knowledge and with an ambition to work in this world of wine.

But really, surely there is life and learning beyond the land of Balzac, baguettes, Bardot and Bordeaux? And there is, as I found out on my student travels round Oddbins in Oxford and to the other side of the world. Back then, I flirted with plenty of wines from other countries, and fell in love with one or two or three or more. In fact, I still love those wines today.

It was as a student in the early nineties that I first tasted and grew to love the wines of Australia and New Zealand, for example. These were big, bold, powerful flavours that were completely new to me: the embodiment in a glass of that thrilling sensation of being somewhere warm and exotic.

The Australian whites in particular were like biting into a perfectly ripe mango with the sticky sweet juice running down my chin, and I just didn't care because that fruit is so gloriously irresistible. And then the oak: the whiff of an old carpenter's workshop – spicy, smoky and exciting.

This was an entirely different experience to tasting the traditional French wines of the sort Uncle Mick and Dad championed (and weaned me on) in their wine bar. As I've said, those French terroir-driven wines are made to taste of the land as much as (if not more than) the grapes they are made from. And they make us work in order to truly appreciate them – they require us to seek out their sometimes elusive, quite particular flavours and aromas.

These new Aussie wines I was discovering were somewhat easier to read. For a start, when I poured them, they literally jumped right out of my glass, screaming, 'I'm here!' and slapping me right around the face with very specific fruit flavours. But also, incredibly helpfully, their labels had the grape variety printed in large letters and, often, right there on the *front* of the bottle. I'd never seen wine labels like that before. Let me explain . . .

I'd grown up with the traditional European way of wine labels: all mystery and history, a few facts and figures, maybe, the ABV – alcohol by volume – and how much wine is actually in the bottle, if you were lucky. And, of course, in my early days in Oxford, it was the old-school French wines, from regions like Châteauneuf du Pape, Corbières, Saint-Émilion, Bourgogne, etc., that you'd find on the shelves of most UK supermarkets. Their labels could be bewildering, like studying a menu presented as lists of villages and vintages rather than what exactly you wanted to eat or drink.

A bottle of Gevrey-Chambertin, for example, although it's made from the Pinot Noir grape, doesn't shout, 'Hey, I'm a Pinot Noir!' In fact, European wine rarely ever has a grape variety printed anywhere on either the front or the back label. Instead, the bottle expects us to know its secrets. Sancerre, the same. The label won't mention Sauvignon, and all these traditional wines are this way – all about place – Rioja, Chianti, Burgundy – like a Geography degree we haven't studied for.

What all these European wines had in common was that they all featured various acronyms which stand for 'appellations', the official classifications of the European wine countries: AOC (France); DO and DOCG (Italy); DO and DOC (Spain); VDP (Germany); DOC (Portugal) . . . the list goes on. The appellation refers to a legally specified area (a named wine region encompassing anything from a couple to many hundreds of hectares) and to gain that appellation, a wine can only be grown and produced in that area which certifies its origin. In other words, you can't just take some red wine grapes, make them into wine in an industrial estate in Croydon or wherever, and then call it Beaujolais, Rioja or Chianti, say.

Additionally, each different European appellation is governed by different rules and regulations about how to make each particular wine, ensuring that everything's done properly and according to tradition, to maintain its character. For example: how vines are grown; which varieties of grapes are grown and in which proportions; how the grapes are harvested; how exactly the wines are made; how and for how long they are aged; their minimum or maximum alcohol content to reach, and much, much more.

The appellation, which is printed on the wine label, is

supposed to help us to understand where and how the wine was produced. But essentially, for most of us, it's like the wine world's secret club and you're only allowed in if you speak wine code – soil types, training methods, aspect ratios, etc. In the early nineties, relative wine novice as I was, a fat lot of help that was for me when trying to decipher hundreds of bottles of these wines marked with AOC/DO/DOC/DOCG, or whatever – labels that didn't give *any* clue as to their grape variety, nor what they might taste like. So, I would stand there in a supermarket, peering at the small print, with no help other than to reference my trusty *Hugh Johnson's Wine Companion*.

Then, in the late eighties and early nineties, came the great Antipodean revolution described above. The Kiwis and Aussies burst in like a sunburst. 'G'day! Mate, forget all that soil and slope business. This is *Chardonnay*!' they announced, making grape varieties the star of the show. Suddenly, wine labels became readable without a PhD in oenology or European geography. They made it simple: *you like Chardonnay? Here's a Chardonnay. Have a go on this – it tastes like sunshine in a glass.* No need to memorise which village in Burgundy makes what. This was *brilliant*!

The very first of these so-called 'New World' wines to hit me round the chops was an Australian Chardonnay, a bottle of Lindemans to be precise, which I bought in the Sainsbury's down by Magdalen Bridge in the centre of Oxford. The oak was about as subtle as a brass band in a library – all buttery toast and cream, with vanilla essence so pronounced it had me looking for the custard creams. That's what oak does to wine and with this bottle of Lindemans, it didn't just complement the Chardonnay, it enveloped it like a warm blanket turning the exotic pineapples into pineapples and cream. Not literally you'll understand but the aromas and flavours I was getting were shimmying a little dance on my tongue and they were all in Hawaiian shirts! And I *loved* it.

For a while then, French wines took a back seat and I looked out for Aussie white wines whenever I set foot in a supermarket. Happily, my local Sainsbury's stocked lots of them. Rosemount Estate, based in the Hunter Valley and South Australia, offered a Chardonnay that tasted like liquidised lemon cheesecake – no need to know about soil types or valley aspects for that one, either. Just 100 per cent in-my-face deliciousness. Mitchelton Reserve, from Central Victoria, took Aussie Chardonnay into Banana-Split Land.

The Aussies, I soon found out, were playing a similar game with their reds – putting the grape varieties in large letters on the front label and coming out with zingers. Just like the Aussie Chardonnays had done for white wine, these Australian reds, made from the Shiraz grape, wafted out aromas and flavours that you didn't need to look for – they came looking for you. They all shared a wonderful ripeness that I hadn't come across before – big, bold fruit flavours that knocked the socks off anything that came out of France. Like Rosemount's Diamond Label Shiraz, for example, a black-pepper-and-blackberry prize fighter with all the subtlety of Tyson Fury – bags full of fruit, masses of spice, and a fairly powerful punch. These red wines didn't need the back-up of food. In fact, far from it. They'd murder any meal I could think of in one sip. Actually, these wines were meals in themselves – bottles to be opened anywhere, anytime and simply enjoyed.

My love affair with these newly discovered flavour-bombs took me out of Sainsbury's in search of new adventures. I started shopping in wine shops, mostly Oddbins on Oxford High Street, where the choice was even greater and where I would spend hours at a time. Stepping inside, my eyes nearly popping out of my head, I felt like Alice tumbling down the vinous rabbit hole. It was chaos – boxes everywhere, hand-written signs stuck at jaunty angles on shelves, bottles crammed into every conceivable space and the wooden floorboards all wonky and creaked – it was all soooo sensual. This was a proper wine shop, with staff who worked there, yes to earn a bit of money, but really because they were wine enthusiasts. A bunch of slightly unhinged professors of plonk.

Here in Oddbins, amongst the organised mayhem and slightly dusty bottles, I first encountered New Zealand Sauvignon Blanc and not just any Sauvignon Blanc, this was Cloudy Bay – the wine that would change everything for me, for a while. Cloudy Bay was one of the greatest Sauvignon Blancs produced in New Zealand – it still is, in fact, although now there are others that are as good if not better. At the time, though, it was an icon. But I didn't just stumble into Oddbins one day and trip over Cloudy Bay. I knew that a shipment had been delivered to the shop and the guys were putting on a tasting that day. A uni lecture on the Weimar Republic or a tasting of Cloudy Bay's latest Sauvignon Blanc release? No prizes for guessing what I chose.

'Forget everything you know about Sauvignon Blanc,' they told me. 'This isn't just wine, it's the new wave of wine. It's changing the game.' And by Christ it was. It tasted like someone had driven a lawnmower through a gooseberry bush then crashed into a pile of ripe passionfruit. It was the most exotic thing I had put in my mouth since the Um Bungo fruit juice my mum used to give me for breakfast. Someone had turned the flavour dial up to eleven and my new-found Aussie Chardonnays were under threat of being shuffled off to the subs bench.

From that day on, the whole Oddbins shop seemed to expand and my horizons followed. They were the Primal Scream of the wine world, presenting wine in a way that no other shop was yet doing and giving me a thirst for all of it – knowledge, bottles and all the stories and magic that came with them.

My weekly visits became a ritual. I'd browse the shelves, *Hugh Johnson's Wine Companion* in hand, picking up bottles, reading labels, learning the language of wine regions and grape varieties. Chilean Merlots took me to Romanian Pinot Noirs to Zinfandels from California, and all of them unashamedly delicious wines sticking two fingers firmly up to the French and their terroir.

Now the supermarket wine aisles began to look different to me, more like a compilation of greatest hits, with Oddbins stocking the B-sides. These wines were generally more expensive but they also had plenty of student-budget gems, selected by people as excited about them as I was.

For me Oddbins was more than just a wine shop – it was my gateway drug to wine appreciation, teaching me that wine could be fun, unpretentious and exciting. Exactly like my uncle Mick, in fact. But in 1993, during my last year at uni, it was my turn to give *him* a lesson in enthusiasm. One spring evening, Mozza the Morris Minor and I were rattling our way through the Chiltern Hills to his house in Hambleden for dinner, complete with a bottle of my latest obsession rolling around in the passenger footwell: Hunter's Sauvignon from Marlborough, New Zealand. This was a high-risk game,

I knew. I was taking a bottle of a very French grape variety grown on the other side of the world to my self-professed Francophile uncle.

Uncle Mick and Aunty Lin's home was just like the wine bar – a temple to French elegance. And they even had their very own vineyard at the end of the garden. As I parked Mozza on their gravel drive, the smell of Lin's chicken casserole wafted through the windows, all herbs and garlic and promise. She was and is a magnificent cook. I walked up to their front door, my bottle of Hunter's Sauvignon Blanc wrapped in white tissue paper. I was so excited to show Uncle Mick my new discovery and to tell him what I'd been up to and what wines I had tasted. He greeted me with his usual broad smile and big hug. He could see the bottle in my hand and he could sense my eagerness as I handed it to him, feigning surprise, as if I was now teaching him, which I wasn't of course.

'What have we got here, Tom?' he asked, knowing full well what we had here.

'Can we taste it?' I said.

With the first pour – all gooseberries, mango and passionfruit – Uncle Mick's nose twitched like he'd just walked into a public urinal.

'This smells like fruit juice,' he exclaimed, not pulling his punches. Then he disappeared into his cellar and emerged with a bottle of Sancerre by Domaine Bailly-Reverdy, also Sauvignon but grown in the Loire Valley in northern France (where they *never* put the grape variety on the label, remember?)

Holding up his bottle like a teacher about to deliver an important lesson to the class, he said, 'Now then, Tom. *This* is how I think Sauvignon Blanc should taste. But we're not going to taste it yet. Let's sit for dinner and taste both wines with our food.'

The casserole sat steaming on the table, a proper French affair that strictly speaking, if we were going to drink white, probably demanded a rich Chardonnay from Burgundy. But we were playing a different game it seemed – Uncle Mick's favourite pastime: the 'Why-France-Will-Always-Make-the-Best-Wine-in-the-World' game.

We got more glasses from the cupboard. He poured his Sancerre. I poured my Hunter's Sauvignon. And we tasted them side by side. Mick's wine was pale lemon, almost green in the light, and with none of that leap-out-and-smack-you aroma of my Hunter's Sauvignon. Instead, I was getting delicate notes of gooseberry and freshly cut grass, like the first proper day of spring. And, yes, it was glorious – rich, complex, and thoroughly French. The New Zealand Sauvignon, with its explosive tropical fruit and pronounced herbaceousness, fought with it, like two cats in an alley.

The difference was marked. Where my Kiwi Sauvignon shouted, its French counterpart whispered. The Sancerre had the freshness of the Hunter's but it was altogether more complex, more difficult to describe – elegant and restrained, a tapestry of subtle flavours rather than a fluorescent-fruit billboard. Uncle Mick could see my expression. 'Terroir,' he said, with his inimitable humility and kindness. He wasn't in it to win or to humiliate me. He was more my long-suffering Zen master, understanding why I, in my youthful exuberance might prefer the bold and brash Kiwi Sauvignon, but showing me that there was room for it *and* the Sancerre. Both terrific in their own way, but worlds apart in style.

'You see,' he said, pouring the last of his bottle, 'I prefer Cat Stevens to Motörhead. I can appreciate Motörhead, but I probably couldn't do a whole album. And Tom, you'll get to Cat Stevens in time.'

And with that, a bottle-and-a-half-down before we'd even started eating, Aunty Lin dished out her legendary chicken casserole. There was no way I was driving back to Oxford that night. Instead, I sat back and soaked up Mick's practical knowledge, the likes of which I'd never find in a textbook, or any classroom tasting. I was with the teacher I adored; one who really respected wine, people and history, and who clearly loved seeing the penny drop for me.

I kept on learning, too. By staring first in bewilderment at the laden supermarket shelves, I slowly began to understand how wines spoke to me through their labels. What before had read like messages written by someone who'd had a few too many themselves, now seemed very much more sensible. But the labels only got me some of the way to finding my path in wine. The real secret? Find a good wine shop with staff who speak human rather than fermentation techniques. That's what I had found with my new friends in Oddbins who urged me to try wines regardless of how intimidating the label was.

The truth is, producers have long experimented with how to present their wines to the world. In my career, I've been lucky enough to witness the evolution of that history and learn about it first-hand. Given the Gilbeys' history in the wine trade, when I think of labels, I think of Château Loudenne, which my great-great-great-grandfather Alfred and his older brother Walter had bought in the nineteenth century. And of course, I think of Le Piat d'Or, one of France's biggest wine success stories to date. This was a red wine made for pleasure – slightly sweet and extremely accessible – created in 1978 specifically for the British market by Independent Distillers and Vintners (IDV), of which the Gilbey family firm was now an integral part.

It was, unquestionably, a brilliant concept. They'd done their homework and realised that us Brits found French wine and their labels intimidating. Too dry for our sweet-toothed palates, too austere and, in the case of the reds, often too tannic. And so, this British company invented a wine that the British could understand. Le Piat d'Or was easy to pronounce, sounded sophisticated and it was easy and smooth to drink. It could be enjoyed without too much grimace or challenge – an affordable wine you could always rely on. And throughout the 1980s, it dominated the UK wine shelves.

The bottle design was brilliant. Eye-catching and clear. I remember a bottle being stuck on our kitchen counter at home – distinctively black with its gold medallion logo, looking classy and meaningful, seemingly straight out of some prestigious French château. Customers would walk up and down wine aisles, passing all the traditionally labelled French wines for their bottle of Le 'Pee-at Door'. Everyone wanted a bit of what 'the French adored', and what's so funny is that the French didn't even drink it. They'd never even heard of it. But Le Piat d'Or created that middle ground between the ultra-posh French wines and the wine local village winemakers dispensed to their customers from demijohns and petrol pumps. It gave people permission to drink French wine without having to understand the intricacies of appellations and terroir. I guess it was the wine equivalent of those package holidays to the Costa Brava – not quite authentic, but comfortable and reassuring.

The TV adverts were hilarious too. 'The French adore Le Piat d'Or!' they cried, in that slightly smug way, showing sophisticated French people (probably just Brits in berets) sipping away in elegant settings. Tailormade to make us feel sophisticated and *très français* . . . even if we were slumped on the settee in front of *Coronation Street*.

The genius of Le Piat d'Or was that it didn't try to educate us – it catered to us – or maybe that wasn't, in fact, genius. The secret behind its success was that, yes, this was French wine but with added stabilisers: slightly sweet, very smooth. Compared to those typically French, complex, interesting wines we were used to, the type my Uncle Mick imported for the wine bar – wines that tingled your teeth or threw a carpet of nails over your tongue (but which blossomed with a bit of Dad's home cooking, I hasten to add) – this red was about as threatening as a teddy bear with a hot water bottle. It's hard not to admire what IDV and Gilbeys achieved with Le Piat d'Or, though.

Just as a decade later, in the early nineties, when the Aussies played a similar trick with Chardonnay and Shiraz, and the Kiwis with Sauvignon Blanc, they helped us Brits to understand a whole new sport – the flavour of wine unadulterated by terroir – the clever marketing of Le Piat d'Or, along with its unthreatening personality, encouraged a whole new swathe of people to try wine, perhaps for the first time. Let's face it, people might not have dared brave those supermarket wine shelves before then; wine was too daunting to understand, too expensive a risk and, well, there are a lot of other drinks that are easier to get along with and do, for some, the same job – take a punt on Piat d'Or though and, who knows, before you know it, you might move on to a Bordeaux or a Burgundy.

But just as the Antipodean Chardonnay and Shiraz star was rising, Le Piat d'Or began to wane. It had done a lot of heavy lifting though.

Fast forward to today, and at the ripe old age of fifty-three (or more, depending on when you are reading this book), with two daughters and a son all working in and around restaurants and wine, I'm still discovering completely new wines altogether. I'm also realising that those Aussie and Kiwi wines I enjoyed tasting and drinking back in the early nineties are precisely what my twenty-something kids are now trying to *undiscover*. A wine like Le Piat d'Or would have them running a mile and any bottle labelled with a popular grape variety, like Merlot, Chardonnay, Shiraz or Sauvignon, say, wouldn't get a look in. *Far* too mainstream it seems. In fact, today, as wine growers seek out heritage grape varieties that have been lost in obscurity for decades, the only well-known grape of old that they seem to find acceptable is Riesling, which can be sweet if it's from Germany; dry if it's from Australia or Alsace; and anything else under the sun if it's from any other country that grows it. It's a case of Russian roulette again, which is back with a bang apparently.

The flipside is that I'm now tasting wines made from little-known grapes such as Catarratto and Nerello Mascalese – grapes from Sicily and Sardinia that I had never heard of when I was sniffing around Oddbins where, on a particularly adventurous expedition, I might have been able to find a dozen different varieties. Supermarkets are now brave enough to stock grape varieties I have to look up.

I'm also tasting wines which now identify as 'natural'. I thought all wine was natural but it appears not. These 'natural' wines are made with no chemicals in the vineyard and no interference in the winery. Most of them are like ticking time bombs – akin to sending milk out in bottles before it's been pasteurised. Back in my Oddbins days, rosé wasn't even a thing and now we've got orange wines, too! These are made from green grapes which usually make white wine but fermented with their skins on (hence most of them being listed as 'skin contact') to give the orange colour and a bit of tannin in the wine, as we'd find in reds.

For me, every day is still a school day and this progression makes wine increasingly exciting. But how did we get from Aussie Chardonnay and Shiraz and Kiwi Sauvignon to the natural and orange wines beloved of trendy wine bars today? Well, a key stepping-stone was via South Africa. At the same time as the Aussie, NZ and Chilean wines were revolutionising the UK wine scene, South Africa in the early nineties at last saw the end of apartheid. Like many countries, in protest at the racist regime the UK had pretty much boycotted everything South African. Then, when Nelson Mandela walked free after twenty-seven years' imprisonment and became president, suddenly the floodgates opened to a whole new world of South African wine. Throughout that decade, I was discovering grape varieties that I'd never heard of – Pinotage, South Africa's signature grape, which is a cross between Pinot Noir and Cinsault, for example. And a South African take on Chenin Blanc, which I'd been sure was exclusive to Vouvray, a little town on the Loire in central northern France – one of the most respected regions in the world for producing extremely complex and honeyed white wines made from this grape.

The timing was perfect, really. The Aussies had enjoyed their fair crack at my wallet; the Kiwis had definitely muscled in too. Now a whole new playing field had opened up to me. These SA wines couldn't be accused of being overly sophisticated but they had heaps of energy.

I remember the first time I tasted Kumala, which in the early days was one of South Africa's most popular wines in the UK. As a treat, my housemate had bought a bottle of their red, a Pinotage. It was a complete revelation. Once again, it was so different from anything I had yet tried, with bags of personality, almost meaty, with an abundance of black, spicy fruit.

My first encounter with a South African Chenin Blanc was in 1993. It was a bottle of Arniston Bay. At first it seemed like it was copying the style of my old Aussie favourite, Lindeman's Bin 65 Chardonnay – going heavy on the oak in a slightly clumsy manner – but I couldn't help but love it. In a style that straddled Australia and France, it felt exotic and sophisticated at the same time. And priced just right at around £5, it sat comfortably between a Lindeman's and the 'treat myself' Mâcon Villages that I used to buy from Sainsbury's, also a Chardonnay but, like all good French wines, it didn't tell you it was.

But the big one, the daddy of the South African wine industry, was KWV. Owned by the state and producing the lion's share of South African wine, you could find KWV's Roodeberg red blend – rough and strong but charming at the same time – in many of the shops I frequented. Nederberg, another well-known winery, had their similar Baronne blend. Neither of these was exactly elegant, but they had this wonderful warmth about them that I fell head over heels in love with.

Back then, the quality of these South African wines was variable at best but that was part of their charm. I felt like I was witnessing the birth of something exciting and new. They had heart and character by the bucket-load and, for me, they bridged a gap between the Antipodes and France. They offered that thrill of discovery and the same I'm-not-quite-sure-if-this-one's-going-to-be-any-good vibe that French wines gave me, but with the added excitement of a completely new flavour palette that was totally unique to South Africa. It felt both familiar and adventurous at the same time.

Those wines marked the beginning of something special – for me and for South Africa. Today, when anyone asks me to list the countries that excite me most in the world of wine, South Africa is in the top three . . . with Portugal and Spain in the mix too.

Back in the nineties, though, the South African wines opened my eyes to new possibilities, new flavours, new stories. They had dropped an extremely fun hand grenade into the shelves of Oddbins and all good wine shops. No resting on their laurels for them.

HOW TO READ A WINE LABEL

This is an art that sometimes can still send me into a spin, especially as some wine labels can be like trying to decode ancient hieroglyphics while doing a headstand.

However, there *are* clues as long as you know how to look. That château name in elaborate gothic script? Probably traditional. A label that looks like it was designed by a street artist after a heavy night out? Likely something more experimental. And if there's an illustration of a kangaroo? Well, you can probably guess where that's from.

Here's what I do when reading a wine label:

1. **THE BIG PRINT TEST.** Look for the biggest letters on the label. That'll tell you something about what the producer wants you to taste. If the grape variety is the largest print on the label we're in safe territory. That means the wine grower is giving you a wine that tastes in line with how the grape is known to taste – Sauvignon, very fruity and zippy, like gooseberries for example, or sometimes mango and passionfruit if it's from New Zealand. There might be something on the back label to elaborate more. If, however, the large type on the label is a region – Rioja, Chablis or Chianti, for example, then the wine grower is giving you something that doesn't taste just of fruit but more of the style of this region. There's sometimes a blend of grape varieties and there'll be other stuff going on in the glass too that'll often make the wines more interesting and delicious when they're served with food – there will be stuff that you can smell and taste that relates to the earth it's grown in, the climate it's grown

in and the way the wine's made – the terroir. Rioja, for example, often aged in oak barrels, can smell of vanilla, cloves and cinnamon. Get googling!

2. **THE PRODUCER CHECK.** Keep hold of your phone and do a quick search for:

- The producer's reputation.
- Their general style (traditional or modern).
- Whether they're known for good value or showing off.

3. **THE YEAR/VINTAGE.** The year that the grapes were harvested to make the wine is often printed on the label, and for nearly all bottles, there is a sweet spot. Most wines will taste better a year or two after bottling. Be careful, though. Rarely does a white wine improve with more than five years' bottle age; and a red rarely gets much better beyond its tenth birthday. I say 'rarely' as the greatest wines (often costing £30-plus) have a much longer shelf life.

- White wines: best drunk within five years (unless you're into wines that taste like old books).
- Red wines: ten years . . . unless it's really rock 'n' roll and the storage conditions are right.
- For red wines, especially those from Europe, the quality of the vintage is important. So, when buying a wine from a traditional wine-growing region such as Saint-Émilion in France, look up the year to see how good it was.

4. **THE FINE PRINT.** If you look closely, hidden in the small text on a wine label you might find:

- Alcohol percentage or ABV – a higher number usually means a riper, fuller-bodied wine.
- Specifics next to the region – for example, 'Reserva' on a Rioja bottle means that it's been aged longer than its younger siblings.

Wine Wanker Approved List #4: Ten Favourite Non-French Bangers

(**Hero bottle** – *Cloudy Bay Sauvignon Blanc, Marlborough, New Zealand*)

Avesso Vinho Verde, Leme, Portugal
An utterly charming and gluggable white made with the Avesso grape variety of the Minho region, northern Portugal. I love so much of what is coming out of Portugal now and this is such a great expression of the clean, fresh, elegant Vinho Verde wines. So well made and so well priced, it's a complete joy.

Sauvignon Blanc, Villa Maria Wines, Marlborough, New Zealand
Villa Maria Wines are the benchmark for great-value, great-quality Kiwi Sauvignon. I love both their less expensive 'Private Bin' and the even more intense 'Cellar Selection'. If you want the thunderbolt I got when I first tasted Hunter's Sauvignon Blanc, get hold of a bottle of this Villa Maria Sauvignon Blanc – it's a bit nuts *and* deliciously decadent.

Syrah, Keermont Vineyards, Stellenbosch, South Africa
These guys make lovely wines. Nothing showy, just classy and delicious. My favourite is this humble Syrah, which is far from their most expensive. Full bodied, smooth, slightly spicy and brimming with juicy black fruit, I find it very difficult to stick to just one glass.

Cabernet Sauvignon, Crossbarn, Napa Valley, California, USA
This wine is made by a bit of a legend of winemaking, Paul Hobbs, and it's a fully loaded pleasure bomb made in the typically Napa style – rich, ripe and generous. It's exactly the style of wine I love – no-holds-barred creamy blackcurrant fruit, all sorts of berries in there too, mouth-filling and juicy with enough complexity to keep you coming back for another sip.

Crystallum Peter Max Pinot Noir, Western Cape, South Africa
Yes, you guessed I love Pinot Noir but my criterion for a great wine is that it's got to make me say 'Holy Shit' when I've taken the first sip. This wine does exactly that. It's so ripe, juicy, elegant and generous. I can taste it as I type and just *love* it.

The Flower and the Bee Treixadura, Coto de Gomariz, Ribeiro, Spain
What a glass full of charm and joy this is and what's equally lovely about it is that it's really not expensive. Ribeiro is rapidly rising up the ladder in my favourite wine-producing regions and this white grape, Treixadura, conjures up stone fruit, white flowers and lemon. It's totally yum.

Pinot Noir, Au Bon Climat Winery, Santa Barbara County, California, USA
This is a benchmark Californian Pinot. Soft, elegant and juicy, it's perhaps my tip for the best-value Pinot Noir for your money out there. It's like diving into a mountain of cushions

so whenever anyone pours me a glass of this wine . . . I'm happy.

Valpolicella Ripasso, Corte Giala 'La Groletta', Allegrini, Italy
This is a wonderful wine lost somewhere between the fruity style of Valpolicella and the head banging style of Amarone. They make it by passing the Valpolicella wine over the skins of the Amarone grapes which adds richness and texture to the wine. The result – a full-bodied, smooth, mouthcoatingly generous red that's a safe bet for game, red meat, winter's nights and log fires.

La Masía, Don Miguel Pinot Noir, Marimar Estate, Russian River Valley, USA
This was the first really special American Pinot I tried and I have since learned that I *love* Pinot from the Russian River Valley. I think you will too. It has all the ripeness and softness I expect from California but with an amazing elegance and finesse too. It's a supremely delicious glass of Pinot.

Tinto Pesquera Reserva, Ribero del Duero, Spain
Pesquera are one of Ribero's premier estates and this Tempranillo wine is such good value for the juice. It needs an hour or two in a decanter before unveiling its glory, then it's a sensation of complex blueberry, blackberry and smoke.

5

Business Balls-Ups . . . I've had a few

PRODUCE OF FRANCE

MACON-FUISSÉ

APPELLATION MACON-FUISSÉ CONTRÔLÉE

WHITE BURGUNDY WINE

ALC. 13% BY VOL.  CONTENTS 750 ML

Mise en bouteille par

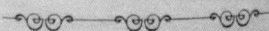

 DOMAINE JEAN-PAUL PAQUET A FUISSÉ - 71960 F

Hero bottle: *Mâcon-Fuissé, Domaine Jean-Paul Pacquet, Burgundy, France*

My early years were wine heavy. Not drinking the stuff but more like living it instead. Wine was ever present in our house, poured at every meal (well, except breakfast, usually) and talked about probably a bit too often. I needed a break. I needed to get on with my life and catch my friends up by earning a bit of money.

It was 1995. While Boyzone and Celine Dion were battling it out in the charts with the Spice Girls, I'd been battling with my bucket of cleaning fluid in a freezing cold winery for a year and a half and, while also studying winemaking at Plumpton College in East Sussex, desperately trying to play catch-up in my Chemistry studies so I might pass the exams and stand some chance of qualifying to become a winemaker.

Beth and I were going strong, but not yet man and wife. Actually, on my then-salary of £9,000 a year, I didn't think we could afford to get married. In fact, if I stayed where I was, I felt I had no real hope of going anywhere. My uni friends had done about as well as I had with their degrees – read 'totally hopeless' – but had managed to land themselves jobs that seemed to get them quite decent pay cheques. All in sales of course – Oliver, who'd failed to get a degree at all, had put watches to one side for now and was flogging copied masterpiece paintings from China; another of our gang, Rob, had sat on the doorstep of a currency broker in London until they got so bored of him they offered him a job; and my housemate Jamie had landed a job selling Champagne (which was all going to run out by the millennium, apparently); Mark (not sure if he did actually get a degree) had set up a business installing jellybean machines in pubs and supplying them with endless refills. They were a right bunch but if they could earn some decent money selling stuff then I thought I could have a pretty good crack at it too.

In fairness, the aforementioned John Worontschak, my boss at Thames Valley Vineyards, had thought I was deranged when I applied to work with him. I had nothing to lose in trying for more, and so I strapped on the parachute and jumped.

I blagged a job with a parcel delivery company – Interlink Express, later part of DPD – on a graduate trainee scheme, no less. They gave me a company car (a tasty white Ford Escort with a magnificent 'whale tail' spoiler on the rear) complete with car phone and a boot jam-packed with sales brochures and presentation packs. I was now a travelling salesman and my mum, filled with more pride than I had ever witnessed (or indeed, was warranted), bought me a pinstripe suit from M&S and a brown faux-leather briefcase (which I've still got to this day in fact).

As sales rep, my job was to convince businesses to use Interlink Express to transport their wares. My designated sales patch was Slough Trading Estate . . . and it really is just like *The Office*. My boss there was just like David Brent and my office was an exact replica of his, Crossbow House. The trading estate is and was massive, almost 500 acres with its own humungous power station as a central feature. It's hideous enough to have our one-time Poet Laureate, John Betjeman, write a poem about it, entitled simply 'Slough'. In my time (and even more so now), you could spend a year on the estate – not that you'd want to – and not see a single bod in a pinstripe suit, let alone carrying a brown briefcase. And yet there I was, sticking out like a sore thumb – me and my white Ford Escort, whale tail and briefcase. Slough was home to all sorts, working for all sorts – over 600 buildings housing about 400 different small, medium and conglomerate businesses from all over the world – mobile phone companies, automobile manufacturers, confectionery makers, welders, electricians... you name it – if they made a widget, I'd want Interlink to shift it. And to make that happen, I'd traipse from one Unit 1A to a Unit 2B, popping my head in at every turn asking to see the boss, and drinking more tea than I could ever have imagined. Soon I became known affectionately as Posh Boy.

'Oi! Posh Boy, you wanna cuppa?'

'Ooh, yes please!' I'd reply.

And along would come my tea served in a mug from some backroom shelf that looked like it had never had a wash. What's more, there always seemed to be a layer of foam at the top of my brew, which was a new one on me. I drank it of course, and, after a while, my tea began to arrive in slightly cleaner cups and the floating foam disappeared. I had made it. And by 'made it', I mean I'd become a small part of the furniture of Slough Trading Estate and, what's more, I loved it. I'd earned my stripes. I'd made good friends all over the estate from receptionists to welders, carpenters to warehouse managers – the lot, and, without exception, they were fantastic. I loved my work, and excuse the brag, at the age of just twenty-five, I became Interlink Express's top sales rep. And with that came a pay rise and a gleaming, brand-spanking-new, silver Rover 200 SE. I felt like a king.

I was now on a salary of £28,000 per year (which, adjusted for inflation, was worth around double this sum in 2025 terms); I had a new company car – and I'd got there with little more than the dubious triple-threat of blind confidence, plenty of ignorance, and just enough humility to preclude actual swagger. Well, maybe a little bit of swagger. I now had a job that actually paid a proper wage, and that perhaps even offered career prospects. And so, with this security, I felt confident enough to pop the big question. And, happily, Beth said yes and we got married in July 1996. More on that later, but for now, the world (well, Slough Trading Estate, at least) was my oyster, and nothing and no one was going to stop me. And then, a few months after our wedding, came the bombshell. A baby. Or rather, Fred. Fred was the bombshell – our eldest of four and the main videographer and editor for every bit of wine content I've put out into the world.

I'd returned from a hard day drinking various cuppas on Slough Trading Estate and Beth had been teaching all day.

'Sit down,' she said when I walked in the door. She was crying, I was nervous and thoroughly confused. Had someone died?

'We're going to have a baby,' she said.

'How? ... NO! ... But *how*?' (read good, naive Catholic boy).

Then, 'What are we going to do?' was all I could muster. The kind of reaction I'm sure every girl craves in this situation.

This is one quite big moment in my life that doesn't have a wine label on it. Probably because I needed something a bit stronger. We were just twenty-five years old. I thought the fun was over. Little did I know that it was just about to start.

At that moment, I couldn't imagine changing our current set-up. We'd struck gold, renting a small flat near Battersea Bridge in south-west London, which we'd both grown to love. Perched on the fourth floor like a bird's nest overlooking the Thames, it was our first home and it was perfect. The bedroom was just large enough for a bed and the kitchen was more of a suggestion than a room – a clever arrangement of essential appliances in which Beth and I developed an intricate dance of cooking movements: 'You stir, I'll reach over you for the wine glasses, pivot left, mind the oven door!' But somehow, we managed to create feasts that I only remember as *magnificent*.

The living room was our pride and joy. It was our cosy nook with aspirations of grandeur, with windows through which we could watch the endless parade of London life flowing across Battersea Bridge down below – red buses glowing like embers in the twilight, cyclists wobbling home after one too many at the old Phene pub, and early morning joggers, of which I was sometimes one, racing their own reflections in the river below. Those windows made it feel like we owned the whole of London. And so we'd arranged our sparse furniture like a game of chess – each piece strategically placed to maximise both the space and the view. Our prized possession was an old leather armchair that had seen better days but was perfectly positioned for watching the sunset paint the river in shades of pink and gold.

The bathroom was what estate agents call 'intimate' and what normal people call 'tiny'. But it had this quirky Art Deco mirror that made it feel like we were actors in a 1920s movie.

What the flat lacked in square footage, it made up for in character. The floorboards creaked, the radiators clicked and groaned, but every square inch held memories: the last stop on a night out for us and many of our friends, somewhere where there was always a bottle of something in the wine rack and a little nibble in the fridge. Here we had hungry midnight feasts, impromptu dance parties on cold winter evenings, watching the rain make patterns on the river, and many a badly-behaved dinner party, all accompanied with generous amounts of wine, of course.

Small in size but huge in heart, it was where Beth and

BUSINESS BALLS-UPS... I'VE HAD A FEW

I had learned to live together, and now someone else was joining our party. The news meant that we'd have to say goodbye to this flat, our first home. Our comfortable little world had suddenly been turned upside down. It was time to grow up. And move on.

While some would have taken this as their sign to stick with the devil they knew, I swung the other way. It was now or never. I had to take my chance in the world I loved, with a product I must surely be able to sell just as well as – even better than maybe – Interlink parcel delivery services. So, I sent my CV to all the wine merchants I knew of, and luckily enough, back came some offers for interviews. I was in for a bit of a shock though.

My first interview was with Corney & Barrow, a traditional London wine merchant that also owns wine bars and acts as the UK agent for two of the most expensive wines in the world: Château Petrus and Domaine de la Romanée Conti. I was fifteen minutes or so into my grilling and things were trundling along quite nicely, I thought, and then came the topic of money.

'We'd be offering a salary of £14,000. Does that work for you?' said one of my potential employers.

I couldn't believe it. Were they serious? Did they think I had some secret stash coming in from another source? I may have been Posh Boy on Slough Trading Estate but I had no family fortune to rely on – this was the nineties, not the 1850s. I blustered my way through the rest of the interview and hoped that they hadn't clocked how despondent I'd become when the subject of money had reared its head.

But thankfully, along came another interview, then another, and then a few job offers. They all seemed to like someone who thought he could sell – no surprises there – but not enough to offer him reasonable pay or an attractive commission package. The offers topped out at £18,000 (equivalent to about £37,000 today) which, even then, made it a big stretch to live in London as a family of three. (Eventually, we'd become a family of six: our twins Georgia and India were born in 1999, and youngest son Billy followed in 2003.) And to top it all, Beth had been fired from her teaching job – for getting pregnant. (It seems HR had not yet become a 'thing' in 1996.)

And then I met Jack Scott, he of the green Bentley fame and the man who changed my life. Without doubt the biggest character I'd ever met. At thirty-five, he cut an imposing figure – like a rugby player who'd discovered good tailoring. Larger than life and completely hilarious, he had piercing arctic-blue eyes that missed nothing and a foghorn laugh that made everyone in earshot want to pull up a chair and share in the joke. He was theatrical without even trying to be and his every gesture and comic timing would have his audience, often me, gasping for air between fits of laughter. In the wine trade, where characters are as varied as the vintages they sell, Jack was definitely a Grand Cru – impressive on paper and even more so in person.

This gregarious bon vivant had started his business, Jascots Wine Merchants, in 1990 and had been happily sourcing and shipping wines, largely from France, and selling them to his customers via the tried-and-tested, no-frills formula of a crammed-full Rolodex contact card-file and a list of great wines typed on two sheets of A4 paper, stapled together, and boom! Hit the telephone . . . hard.

All Jack's customers loved him and included some of the

biggest wine buyers in London – top restaurants and catering companies, and the big City law firms and international banks, whose offices boasted in-house chefs and grand dining rooms in which to host clients – really, some of the best. And while the other companies I'd interviewed for boasted glossy sales brochures full of beautiful colour photographs of dusty bottles, crusty winemakers and gorgeous-looking ancient oak barrels, not to mention swanky uptown offices and frightfully important-looking people running things and working for them, there was Jack, solo, nailing business from his modest office in Hammersmith with his old-school telephone and his ever-evolving list of contacts in his jam-packed Rolodex. And he offered me a job there and then. No mobile phone, no company car, no cosy clients to start selling to, no fancy brochures, no smart office in St James's, and I'd have to share a desk with Ian, the delivery driver. If this job was going to be anything, it had to be all about the wines.

So, before I accepted his job, I asked Jack if I could taste his selection. I knew what a good Sancerre should taste like; I knew a good Fleurie when I tasted one; and a good Rioja too, so we agreed that I'd come back to his Hammersmith HQ one day the following week. Jack would line up all the wines I wanted to taste and we would run through them together.

'Dear boy!' he boomed, as I walked up the stairs to his office, his voice filling the room like good port fills a glass – rich, warm and generous.

When I say office, it was one small room which housed three desks – a big one for Jack, a slightly smaller one for Charlie, his pub salesman (and my great friend who introduced me to Jack in the first place), and an even smaller one for Ian the delivery driver. In the middle was a worn old butcher's block, normally covered in delivery notes, but now displaying eight bottles of wine awaiting my judgement.

'Now,' Jack said, rubbing his hands together with the glee of a man about to share his favourite party trick, 'we'll start with something to wake up the palate. Nothing too serious yet – we're not barbarians who dive straight into the heavy reds before noon!'

Now, I should add here that Jack didn't and doesn't drink alcohol. As he would say, he'd 'had his allocation' – a common situation in the wine trade. Working in the 'sweety shop' is hard for all us wine trade folk and we have to manage it in the way that works best for each of us. It didn't suppress any of his energy and enthusiasm though – I was getting Jack Scott, spittoon by his side, *full throttle*.

He reached for a bottle of Champagne and announced, 'You know what they say – you can't trust a wine merchant who doesn't love Champagne!'

The pop of the cork was the starting pistol for what would turn into a three-hour masterclass in not just wine, but in how to share it with enthusiasm and joy.

Jack had judged the order in which we tasted the wines perfectly, yet it didn't feel staged or pretentious. He had the rare gift of making precision feel like spontaneity, expertise feel like shared discovery. And he didn't just pour his wines – he introduced them like cherished friends at a party. And the wines themselves? They weren't just good, they were outstanding. Each a great example of how the particular appellation *should* taste, but with just that extra bit of either power, finesse or elegance. I'd never come across wines like these before. The Fleurie was a wine who'd put on her silk dress and gone jiving. It was like drinking a distillation of crushed

BUSINESS BALLS-UPS... I'VE HAD A FEW

strawberries and rose petals. Next a Sancerre, fresh like a summer morning in the Loire. Then a Pouilly-Fumé, then a Chilean Cabernet Sauvignon, and so on and so on. Yes, the wines were special but even more special was Jack. Each new bottle came with a story; each wine with an anecdote about the producer, the vintage, or some memorable occasion when he'd shared it. They were part of his life story.

Why, though, I wondered, had he opened the Saint-Émilion for tasting before I arrived?

'Because, Tommy,' Jack replied, 'this Saint-Émilion is a bit like a Parisian waiter – it looks down its nose at you for the first hour, then turns out to be your best friend by the end of the night!'

By the end of the tasting my head was spinning, infused with excitement. I'd obviously not learned much from my escapades in the Hunter Valley in Australia as, once again, I don't think I spat much out. Jack then looked at me with that twinkle in his eye I'd grow to know so well and asked, 'Well, boy, what do you think? Do you want the job?'

How could I not want to work for this man who'd just transformed my understanding of what wine was and could be?

'You reckon you can sell these?' Jack continued. 'I'll pay you £9,000 plus 10 per cent commission on whatever you sell.'

OK, I know what you're thinking. £9,000 was taking me back to the salary I was on when I was single, living at home and working at Thames Valley Vineyards. I'd also turned down similarly low-paid jobs at three posh City wine merchants, one of whom my uncle Mick had said I'd be crazy *not* to take. But I knew I could sell, and I knew Jack's wines were good. What's more, I could see what he had achieved with just his contact list and a phone – I was sure I could do the same. I'd done the sums and I knew that once my commission was loaded on top, I could get that £9,000 up to at least what I'd been earning at Interlink Express, if not more. Plus, *these wines* – and Jack – had simply knocked my socks off. Anyone who could make eight glasses of fermented grape juice feel like a ticket to the best show on earth was someone I needed to learn from.

So, I backed myself. My first job in the big bad wine trade in London. The place where it really happened for me.

While in my head I quickly began listing all the people I knew who'd buy Jack's wines – all Dad's friends, all Beth's parents' friends, all my friends' parents – he handed me a £20 note and said, 'Welcome, boy. Now, get yourself down to Blackwell's and buy a directory of all the Public Limited Companies in London. Loads of them have their own dining rooms, the directors drink shedloads, and you'll be perfect with them. Get on with it.'

I duly skipped off to the bookshop in Holborn, bagged my directory, and readied myself for my first day's work at Jascots. The following Monday morning, 8.30 a.m. sharp, I opened the book, started on the As, and began dialling. My task was to sell a Mâcon-Fuissé made by Jean-Paul Pacquet. Jack had recently shipped over two pallets (600 bottles) of this white wine from Burgundy, the Mâconnais region to be precise, very near Beaujolais and thus near Lyon. It oozed richness, creaminess and class, with the citrusy, lemony tang of the best of these wines, and it even went one step further: it added a layer of Werther's Originals – that tiny hint of butterscotch that made it just sooo moreish. Not sweet, just citrusy, creamy and rich – like a scallop fried in salt-crystallised butter. And we were selling it at £7.95 per bottle including delivery and VAT. A bargain.

Thanks to my days on Slough Trading Estate with Interlink Express, I'd become quite thick-skinned. I didn't mind people putting the phone down on me. So, using my killer opening line of, 'I wonder if you can help me?' by about 11 a.m., I'd booked my first meeting – with an insurance company called AON.

On day two, I hit the phone again and set up ten more meetings. I was all set to start wearing out my Hush Puppies, clutching a corkscrew and my cool bag packed with my sample bottle of Mâcon-Fuissé.

The weeks went by in a happy flurry of phone calls and rushing around the City, selling wine and winning customers, many of whom became good friends. In that first year with Jack, and from a standing start, I sold £700,000 worth of wine; in my second, £1.3 million. And within three years, the boss decided to change the rules. Jack made me his business partner, and so began ten more years of laughter and adventure. I believed in myself, and I believed in us. We could identify good wine, and we could sell it – both of us. My travels took me beyond the directory of public limited companies to some of London's top restaurants, event-catering companies and even to the Oxford and Cambridge colleges. There was no one and nowhere I wouldn't have a crack at – if they bought wine, they'd get a call from me.

That's how in the early days of my salesman career, one crisp, spring Tuesday back in 1999, I found myself scuttling through the quad of St John's College, Oxford, and towards one of the finest cellars in the land. St John's is the wealthiest of all the Oxford colleges, with assets worth well over £700 million, and its cellar alone was insured for over £3 million, so I was told later, although at the time I hadn't a clue. This was just another blunder into the unknown, the result of a cold call to the college's fabulously eccentric head of wine for the Buttery (the student dining rooms), Paul Ashman.

Despite living in Oxford as a student, this world of the Oxbridge colleges was a whole new and very strange world to me, one that makes Hogwarts seem positively pedestrian. I was to discover that every college has a head of wine for the students and most colleges have a wine steward to choose wine for the fellows. The buyer for the students would buy for college parties, the student canteen and the bar – the wine that needed constant replenishment – while the wine steward would often buy the posh stuff – the wines for the college cellar. The wine steward would look down his nose (and it was always 'his' in those days – they were all men) in distaste at my wine list, photocopied on two sheets of A4 paper, while he decided whether or not to take pity on me and give me an order. The buyers for the parties and students on the other hand never had time to read any wine list – people were barking orders and questions at him (and again it always *was* him) from breakfast to bar time.

Paul, the buyer for the St John's students, seemed to only enjoy one moment of quiet every day – from 11 a.m. for forty-five minutes, to be precise. But it was him I was after, the master of the engine room that needed to be constantly refuelled with everyday wine – i.e., not the *really* posh stuff that had to spend ten years in a cool, dark, damp cellar before the label fell off and I could take another order.

'I'll be in Oxford next Tuesday,' I had suggested, 'would

you mind if I popped in to pour you a delicious glass of Bourgogne Pinot Noir by Bertrand Ambroise?'

'Yes, why not?' he'd replied, amiably. 'Eleven a.m. I can't see you before then.'

Kerching!!

Of course, I had no reason to be in Oxford that Tuesday. And if he'd said Tuesday was no good, I was ready with Wednesday, Thursday or Friday, 'as I'm around Oxford for most of the week.' Very casual, very calm and just cross my fingers for a 'yes'. And when the 'yes' came, I'd immediately follow up, scribbling a hand-written note saying, 'Thanks and can't wait to meet you at 11 a.m. on Tuesday,' or something to that effect, then pop it in the post. Old school tactics, which made me stand out, and which I urge all paperless folk to employ today. It's the nudge that fixed me and my meeting in my various prospects' memory. Also, it put the onus on them to call me and cancel if something came up as there was no easy reply by email, and it worked; they'd pretty much always be there when I turned up.

On the Tuesday at the appointed hour, I did turn up . . . on my Ferrari-red 1998 Triumph Thunderbird Sport. Yes, another good thing about this new job was that I got a company vehicle. No car but rather this beautiful (looking and sounding) motorbike. It was the perfect transport for a family of three with a new baby! A stunning British machine, complete with gleaming silver exhaust and a very handy tank bag, ideal for transporting six bottles of fine Burgundy – fast – an essential bit of kit for a new wine salesman who needed to cram in as many tastings as he could in a day. And no surprise, it got me a few orders. My customers loved the Triumph (Beth perhaps less so). Some even asked me to take them for a spin on the back and my favourite restaurant customer christened it 'The Gents' Express'.

That Tuesday, I pulled up outside the porters' lodge in my leathers. Then a quick change behind the bike: off with the leather trousers, a moment shivering in my boxer shorts, then on with my suit trousers (from my left pannier). Gather the Bourgogne Pinot Noir (and a handful of other more grown-up wines, just in case), a quick swish of the hair, then into the lodge to register my arrival. I'd never been inside an Oxford college before, and when I stepped through the ancient wooden door my jaw hit the floor. To me it was a portal to mystery and magic, closely guarded by this cuddly-looking man – the very amiable lodge porter. Pigeonholes crammed with each student's mail, notices all over the walls about the various magic and potion lessons going on that week, instructions to all students about how to put their pants on, and generally the hub of everything going on in college. I'd never seen anything like it before, this arcane, oddly anachronistic, ultimately exclusive club with its own way of working, quite different to my usual world of chefs, dining rooms, restaurants and night clubs.

'Into the quad, through Gate K, then carry on to the refectory,' the porter instructed with various hand signals.

So off I strode, into the most beautiful, haunting quad, empty but for me, minding not to step on the grass, and down the ancient corridor into the refectory. But where was my potential customer? Where was anyone in fact? In a wavering voice, I started calling . . . 'Mr Ashman? Mr Ashman?'

'Yes?' came a faint reply from somewhere over by the corner of the kitchen. 'Come down.'

I followed the voice through a narrow arch, which led

to a set of cold, damp stone steps. Paul Ashman was down in the cellar putting wine away, naturally. Health and safety was clearly not a priority here and these steps were not made for anybody over 5'5" – and on a good day, I'm 6' 2". But gingerly down the narrow staircase I crept, the temperature steadily dropping until there, at the end of one of the dark aisles, was Paul, almost drowning in wine. Before me was the most substantial collection of wine I have ever laid eyes on. The cellar was ram-packed with bottles – like a hoarder's lair. Still to this day, I have never visited a wine cellar quite as impressive, and I've seen a fair few... The wealthiest, stuffiest clubs in London? They've got nothing on this. Nor had I ever smelt a cellar like this one at St John's College. The cellars I knew in France were full of barrels of wine – some fermenting, some maturing, some empty and cleaned, ready for the next harvest – and so smelt like wine. This cellar smelled like it felt – musty and damp.

As I made my way through the racks to reach Paul, I was stepping over imperials (6-litre bottles) of Château Latour and magnums of fine Burgundies all waiting to be unboxed and put away. Heaps and heaps of truly extraordinary wines. Some of their names I'd only dreamed of ever seeing, in fact – Latour being one of the most expensive wines of Bordeaux and, therefore, the world. I was like a kid at the pick 'n' mix counter.

Then, spotting three other serious-looking chaps standing along with Paul, all already tasting wine and ready to taste more – my bottle of Pinot Noir from Burgundy – all excitement turned to terror. Paul introduced them as the (relatively new) college wine steward, Dr Ian Sobey, a professional hockey player and brilliant Professor of

Mathematics; the money man aka the college bursar; and Stephen G. Davies, the pioneering Professor of Chemistry. These incredibly important, highly intelligent and, as I later appreciated, extremely kind and funny people, had given up their valuable time to taste wine with me – a bit of a chancer who, as yet, had no reputation to speak of in the wine world. I would soon find out that this, an 11 a.m. tasting to select wines for that week's upcoming feasts, was very much the norm. They'd meet down in the cellar to pull out dusty old bottles bought years ago by previous wine stewards, taste them and decide whether to keep the others for a bit longer, or bring them out to play. Me and my Pinot Noir from Burgundy were a little game at the end and I'd got here by a cold call.

In time I got to know and like Ian (Dr Sobey) immensely. A born entertainer, straight out of central casting – 'Oxford don, slightly eccentric, wine enthusiast' – except that he was an Aussie, but with all the other requisites, including leather elbow-patches and a battered bow tie that could have witnessed every single spring ball since 1962.

About a year after our first meeting, he called me in a state of great agitation.

'Tom, Tom . . . you've got to get in here. All my white Burgundy's faacked!'

Dr Sobey had inherited the cream of white Burgundy wines in that cellar – bottles of Meursault and Puligny-Montrachet galore, from the very best growers. When I got there, we tasted together and he was right: many of these bottles, mostly from the 2002 vintage and particularly the more expensive wines, were indeed 'faacked'. It was a bit of a disaster, because in today's money, recent vintages of these same wines in an 'unfaacked' condition would cost you upwards of £150 a bottle, and he had a lot of them.

We continued to taste, selecting random bottles from the different growers and sure enough, about one in every seven or eight bottles was 'maderised' – when oxygen somehow gets into the wine making it turn darker, more orange-like in colour, and spoiling its flavour by giving it a definite whack of marmalade rather than the vibrant, complex fresh citrus and tropical fruit of a white Burgundy in good nick. So, the situation we had here was that he was long on white Burgundy of which a significant proportion was well and truly 'faacked' (far too many bad bottles to risk serving it at a college dinner); and Jack and I were long on big Aussie Shiraz which was sitting gathering dust in our warehouse – none of our punters wanted it any more... And so came the best Christmas sale I have ever made. We boxed up *all* his potentially 'faacked' white Burgundy and swapped it for some of our very decent Aussie Shiraz. It was a good deal because the only other place his white Burgundy was going was down the sink. It was good for me too because I boxed it all up and sold it by the case at £10 a bottle, with strict instructions to drink it by Christmas... and I didn't want to hear back from anybody unless more than four bottles were off in each case of twelve. I had averaged that you'd get two knackered ones in twelve but the other ten would be stellar so I had very happy customers all round. They were getting bottles of wine that would otherwise have cost more like £70 and a fun game of Russian Roulette thrown into the bargain.

I learned so much working with Jack. We met and won

some great customers and had so many adventures. Adventures in business more than with wine, really, although they certainly involved wine. Early on I learned about 'credit'. We were a small business and ran everything on trust. Jack trusted me not to do business with bandits and I trusted my customers not to be bandits. So, we delivered our wine to customers then they'd pay us, thirty days after the date of invoice. One day, I came across a seemingly lovely man running a busy wine bar in South Kensington. He seemed like the archetypal British gent but he turned out to be one of the biggest bandits I've ever delivered wine to. When he refused to pay us, Jack got so fed up he bundled me into the delivery van and we swiped all his furniture . . . which got us paid pretty quickly of course.

And sometimes the stakes were higher . . .

It was 6.30 a.m. on a grey Tuesday in 2005 and I had whizzed by the office early to collect a few things I needed for an event I was hosting that evening on an island off Cannes in the south of France for one of the big City property firms – bottle covers to hide the wine labels, aroma wheels, and all the other fun gizmos I use for a blind wine tasting. Next stop was Gatwick to catch my flight to Nice.

Just as I was locking up again my phone buzzed. It was the customer-turned-good-friend from the firm I was going to meet. You'd be hard pushed to meet a more composed, kind and thoughtful man but now he was gabbling at me, ten to the dozen.

'Don't get on the flight,' he screamed. 'We're going under. The liquidators are coming to clear us out so you need to come *now* and get your wine.'

We'd recently delivered about £50,000 of wine to the firm

which had not yet been paid for. This big order, now sitting in the cellar underneath their head office, had been the cornerstone of my sales figures for that quarter and if I didn't move fast, it, and the unpaid invoice, were about to disappear into the liquidator's hands.

Still catching his breath, he continued, 'I think I can keep them upstairs while they are counting paperclips up here in the office, so that should give you about an hour to clear out the cellar.'

Our delivery drivers started loading their vans at six each morning, so they were all downstairs preparing for their day. I jumped down the stairs in threes, ran to our warehouse manager, tried to explain the situation calmly and asked him desperately if I could grab one of the drivers.

Thank goodness, our super calm warehouse manager, an ex-sergeant major, was exactly the man I needed in this situation. He was the kind who'd help you bury a body and not ask questions.

'Simon and Malcolm,' he shouted. 'You've got a new mission. Give me your loading sheets. You're going out with Tom.'

Within five minutes of that call, me, two drivers and a van were on the road. The City was just waking up when at 7.15 a.m., we pulled up outside the office in Threadneedle Street. All the while my phone was pinging with texts to and from my target. I knew exactly where the entrance to the cellar was and he'd sent me the key code. And I was in. That cellar was something else. I'd spent months stocking it with exactly what the firm needed to impress its clients – cases of Château Talbot, Château Latour and more; magnums of Krug, Sassicaia, Vintage Taylor's Port . . . a golden stash and we had an empty van to load it in. Simon backed up to the cellar door, like a getaway driver in a heist movie or *Mission Impossible* on steroids.

I could hear people talking and moving about upstairs in the office.

'Form a chain,' hissed Malcolm, as I carried the first two pristine wooden cases of Bordeaux up the narrow cellar stairs. Together, we worked in near silence, passing boxes hand to hand up and into the back of the van. I can still feel the weight of those wooden cases, smell the musty cellar air mixed with the tobacco breath of Simon and Malcolm. In each corner of the cellar, I'd spot another bottle that I needed to rescue – that last case of Pol Roger Sir Winston Churchill . . . Every footstep echoed; every clink of bottles made me wince; a few early-bird suits walked by, but this was the City: all action at all hours and this looked totally normal.

By 8.30 a.m. we were done. I carefully shut and locked the cellar door, jumped back into the van, one turn of the key and we were off. We'd rescued the whole lot.

The next day, the financial pages reported the firm's collapse, but by then the wine was safely stored on a special shelf in our warehouse, even if my nerves were shot to pieces. Every single precious bottle accounted for, though I didn't hear again from my friend in the City for a good few weeks. For many years that salvaged hoard sat gathering a bit more dust, reminding me of that dawn phone call, the warehouse manager's unflappable calm, and the sound and smells of that cellar in the City. Every now and then, I'd dig out a bottle from that heist – Château Talbot 2005 – and share it with my good friend, the whistleblower. It's complete nectar that tastes even better for its journey.

But the drama didn't always involve fine wine and non-payments – sometimes it was a matter of some very, very ordinary wine...

If you've ever wondered what pure panic looks like, it's my face, turned sheet-white, sitting on the Tube on the morning of Thursday 2 December, 2007 having just received a text from an events manager who wondered why he was a few hundred wine cases short for a number of imminent Christmas parties – the very next week. Not just any events manager, but *the* events manager of Evolution London, the catering and events company in Battersea, which put on the most and the biggest Christmas parties in town. This fellow was responsible for handling parties for more than 5,000 guests every night during December.

I leapt off the Tube at the next station and quickly dialled his number. He picked up before the first ring had even ended, his voice cracking with anxiety. They were missing 3,000 bottles of the specific Spanish white and red wine, called Las dos Marias, that they'd promised to serve at every single Christmas party his company had lined up. Wines which their clients had pre-approved, which they had printed on all their menus, which by now should have arrived on a shipment direct from the Spanish winery, and which they absolutely couldn't substitute at such short notice. They *had* to serve it to thousands of corporate revellers in just a few days' time. In short, running out of this wine was like Father Christmas running out of presents.

As I continued my journey, the panic escalated. By the time I reached Earls Court, I had Evolution London's big boss on the line, his tone very direct. This was *not* my cock up, I tried to argue, but he seemed to think that it might be. I did some quick maths – three vans could carry two pallets each, that was 1,200 bottles per van. If they left Hammersmith that evening and made a mad dash through France and into Spain, they could be at the Las dos Marias winery for Friday evening, and then assuming the wine was even available, they could make it back to Blighty for Sunday night. This was the sort of logistical nightmare that would get my ex-sergeant-major warehouse manager proper excited.

Thankfully, we'd bought so much wine from this bodega over the years that when I called the head honcho, he didn't laugh me off the phone. 'Yes, Tom, we have the wine,' he said, 'but our warehouse closes at four p.m. on Friday.'

What followed was the biggest scramble I'd yet instigated and it involved three transit vans, complete with three of our most trusted drivers, and enough Red Bull to float a battleship. The plan was simple: drive to Spain, load up with the wine, drive back. Do it in three days or Christmas was ruined for many excited partygoers – and I'd be going down with the ship.

I can still picture the drivers as they pulled out of our warehouse yard at 2 p.m. that Thursday, destination loaded on satnavs, and armed with the hastily prepared paperwork needed to collect and clear customs, the bodega contact details, and my credit card for emergencies. 'Don't worry, boss,' our brilliant lead, an ex-con from Poland whom I'd trust with my children, dog, and all my passwords assured me, 'we've got this. Spanish wine runs are like a holiday compared to dealing with the City traffic.'

The next seventy-two hours were a blur of text messages and tracking updates. The vans made it most of the way down through France in good time, then somewhere south

BUSINESS BALLS-UPS... I'VE HAD A FEW

of Bordeaux one developed a worrying rattle. Still, they pressed on. They arrived as the clock ticked towards the 4 p.m. cut-off to find that the bodega's forklift wasn't charged. Every hour brought a new crisis but somehow they did it and the three vans, and 3,600 bottles of Spanish hooch, started to rattle their way back across Europe. The valiant convoy arrived back at the warehouse at six on the Sunday morning. Admittedly, the drivers all looked like they'd aged ten years but they were proud as punch, grinning like schoolboys who'd just pulled off the ultimate prank.

The Las dos Marias wine itself? Well, it was nothing special at all – a decent enough glugger that tasted as good out of a coffee cup as it did from a Riedel sommelier glass... But at that moment, as we unloaded those vans in the dark December daybreak, it was more special to me than any Vega Sicilia (possibly the most expensive Spanish wine) could ever be. Each case we stacked was another Christmas party saved. Another disaster averted.

When the boys delivered it to the venue the next day, I swear we had the head of operations weeping. Proper tears of relief. They'd already started rehearsing how they'd explain the cock up to goodness knows how many corporate managers.

The funny thing is, of all the wines I've sold over the years – the fine Burgundies, the vintage Champagnes, the cult California Cabernets – it's that Las dos Marias cheapo Spanish grog that stands out in my memory. Not because of how it tasted, but because of what it represented: that sometimes in our wine world, it's not about what's in the bottle, but about getting those bottles where they need to be. About the comfort of a promise made to a group of valued employees.

Greg and his team became legends after that. Any time they delivered to that company again they were given a meal and any time a fellow driver complained of a difficult delivery, they'd invite him to drive to Spain and back the next weekend. That tended to shut the moaner up pretty quick.

I've still got a few bottles of that Las dos Marias wine. Why, I'm not sure, but when I last opened one it tasted deliciously foul. I'm sure I detected a whiff of diesel but it reminds me of victory, and so to me it's delectable all the same.

HOW TO START AND GROW A WINE COLLECTION

Building my own wine collection has been one of my greatest joys – especially as, when I pull a bottle out to drink, it's as good as free because I can't remember having paid for it – any financial pain is too far in the past to remember it.

But collecting wine has also been the source of some of my greatest disappointments: when I've left a bottle too long on the rack and it's lost some of its joy. Or when it's just not as good as I remembered or expected it to be.

If you're keen on wine, though, you should give it a go. You don't need a massive cellar, just any cool and dark space. And, sometimes, you can keep the wine in storage with the merchant you bought it from.

Here are some tips:

- Don't buy too many bottles. Have an idea of what you might use during a year and buy accordingly.

- Taste before you buy. Don't trust anyone's recommendations or palate (even mine) other than your own.

- Buy from places or tastings you've enjoyed, and from people you like. Wine should bring back good memories.

- Buy more red wine than white or rosé – generally speaking, red wine benefits more from ageing than most whites and rosés.

- Keep track of what you've got stashed away and if in doubt, drink it. It's much better to drink wine too young than too old.

Wine Wanker Approved List #5: Ten Favourite Chardonnays

(**Hero bottle** – *Mâcon-Fuissé, Domaine Jean-Paul Pacquet, Burgundy, France*)

Danbury Ridge Chardonnay, Essex, England
Grown in Essex, one of the warmest areas in the UK, this is a tribute to just how far England has come in making white wines. This Chardonnay holds its own admirably alongside white wines from Burgundy at double its price. It's such a far cry from English wine as I knew it in the early nineties.

Pouilly-Fuissé, Domaine J. A. Ferret, Burgundy, France
This was my first introduction to the luscious white wines of the Mâconnais in the south of Burgundy – courtesy of my uncle Mick. It was and still is like lemon meringue pie in a glass – fresh citrus but with a layer of vanilla and toffee to it, too. A stand-out wine for me and I think of the old boy whenever it passes my lips.

Auxey-Duresses, David Moret, Côte de Beaune, Burgundy, France
Auxey-Duresses isn't nearly as famed as Meursault, Chassagne-Montrachet or Puligny-Montrachet but when you put winemaker David Moret there you get a magnificent drop. Look for any wine with this man's name on the label, and you're in for a treat.

BUSINESS BALLS-UPS... I'VE HAD A FEW

L'Étoile Organic Chardonnay, Domaine Begude, Limoux, France
If you like Chardonnay, you've got to try some from Limoux in the south of France. They have some crackers and Domaine Begude wines are right up there with the best. This is creamy and bursting with multiple layers of deliciously fresh citrus fruit but, as is the way with Limoux, they somehow manage to get a bit of nuttiness in there too.

Chardonnay, Hamilton Russell Vineyards, Hemel-en-Aarde Valley, Hermanus, South Africa
This would have nine out of ten of us thinking it was a very good white Burgundy Chardonnay from France because it has all those classic traits – balance, finesse and elegance. But it somehow manages to spread an extra layer of unctuousness in there too. It fills the mouth and is, well, really really tasty. Try the Hamilton Russell Pinot Noir, too – it's another cracker.

Pouilly-Fuissé 'Vieilles Vignes', Domaine Cordier Père et Fils, Burgundy, France
I love Cordier's rich and generous white wines. They're all citrus fruit and butter with elegance and class. A real proper mouthful of decadence but don't serve it too cold – it'll mask some of the wine's generosity and texture.

Mâcon-Vergisson, Domaine des Deux Roches, Burgundy, France
I think these guys have a secret stash of Werther's Originals in the barrel room as all of their wines have an unmistakable

delicious smack of toffee to them. If you're thinking supermarket Mâcon Villages when reading this, think again. This is fully loaded white Burgundy of the highest quality and you'll love it.

Chablis Premier Cru 'Fourneaux', Samuel Billaud, Chablis, France
This man really is the master of Chablis and his wine knocked me sideways when I first tasted it. So pure and elegant with delicious green apple and citrus fruit. Buy any white wine made by Samuel Billaud and you'll be in for a real treat.

Au Bon Climat Wild Boy Chardonnay, Santa Barbara, California, USA
Such an expressive wine this, with rich, ripe, generous fruit whilst retaining the elegance demanded of a really good wine. It's a complete cracker and a must try.

Toques et Clochers 'Haute Vallée' Chardonnay, Limoux, France
This is a fully loaded, ballsy, Burgundian-style Chardonnay at half the price you'd pay if it did actually come from Burgundy. Rich with citrus and buttery notes and a lovely smack of spice.

6
Swordfights & Sommeliers

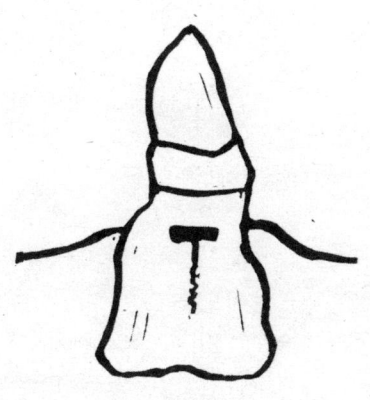

Hero bottle: *Champagne André Clouet Cuvée 1911*

Jean-François Clouet and I first met thanks to his family's Champagne. He'd sent me a bottle of his beautiful fizz in the hope of finding a UK importer. I remember my first taste as if it was yesterday. Its aroma was like a fruit bowl in a bakery – autumnal red apples and pears with a waft of baked brioche – and it tasted as good as it looked and smelled and so, a visit to Jean-François would be the first stop on Jack's and my next French wine-buying tour.

When you appreciate the work and love that go into making great wine, it becomes so much more than the sum of its parts. When you get to know the place or family that made the wine, it's a pretty perfect moment when you open that bottle to pour for friends and family. It makes me want to raise my glass to them and almost always it'll bring me some good memories – happy times and happy adventures. That's what wine can do – yes, too much of it can obliterate all recollection, but just the right amount of the right stuff makes it all flood right back.

And now when I get to pop open a bottle of André Clouet Grand Cru Champagne, I always smile. With its deep, glossy, navy-blue label that shimmers like silk in the light, the gold lettering in that quintessentially ornate French style practically dancing off it, the bottle is one of the most beautiful I've seen. Then to top it all, when you've torn through the rich gold foil around the cork, the capsule features a sepia-toned photograph of Jean-François's great-great-great-something-grandfather, André Clouet, the founder of the estate, complete with handlebar moustache. Even with no Champagne inside, that bottle has to be worth at least £40.

And so, we found ourselves in Bouzy(!), one of the Champagne's seventeen Grand Cru villages and home to some of the finest Pinot Noir vineyards in the region, including the Clouet family estate. And we were searching for Jean-François who would show us around the domaine. We crawled through the quiet, sleepy streets, checking house numbers behind ancient gates and feeling increasingly like we were in the wrong place entirely. There was not a soul in sight; the only sign of life a single fat cat lying sunbathing on a garden wall. Then, just as I was about to suggest that we might be in the wrong Bouzy, we turned a corner to see a very jolly young man bouncing in the middle of the road like Tigger after three double espressos.

'Bonjour!' he exclaimed, and bounded over to the car window.

'You park eeeer,' he suggested and showed us through some rose-covered gates to a small house set in a similarly modest courtyard. To be honest it could have been any pretty house in any quiet, quaint French village, and from the road we couldn't see any vines or winery but, with its pristine gravel drive and rose-scented garden, it was a welcome stop on our travels. 'I 'ave been waiting! Come, come! We drink Champagne for breakfast, yes?'

It was 2.30 in the afternoon, so maybe, I thought, he meant that he'd been on the Champagne since breakfast.

So, *this* was Jean-François. Around the same age as me, and he was already the big boss of the family business. But also, as bonkers as a box of frogs. Back then, on first impressions, he was the kind of guy that made me wonder if growing up surrounded by bubbles did something peculiar to your personality. His English was creative, to say the least, mixing technical wine terms with what seemed to be lyrics from eighties pop songs. 'Zis Champagne,' he'd declare, holding a bottle aloft like Rafiki presenting Simba, 'it 'as ze fine bubbles like... 'ow you say... young and sweet!' Then he'd do a little ABBA shimmy between the tanks.

But before any of that, indeed, before I'd even closed my car door, first it was the tunnels.

'You must see *les tunnels des Nazis*!!' Jean-François announced. This was not the welcome we'd expected from a Champagne producer. The norm was to start with a polite tour of the press house, maybe a peek at the vines, but no, on our first visit to the Clouet establishment, our excitable host wanted to show us where his family had hidden their best wines from the Nazis during the occupation.

We walked to the side of the house where JF (as I'll now call him for short) opened a small, creaky, wooden door. When he switched on the light inside, we saw before us some steep narrow steps, carved out of the rock, leading down into the cold and damp chalk cellars – all gothic shadows and history. 'Mind out your 'eads,' he told us as we followed him down. At the bottom, he pulled out a torch and pointed it at what looked like a solid wall. 'My grandfazza built false walls and sealed them with chalk so the Germans never found our good stuff!' He bounced around, beaming with pride, as if he'd hidden the wines down there himself.

Back upstairs, he led us into the house and to the tasting room for a masterclass in both Champagne and theatrics, his parents popping their heads in occasionally looking simultaneously proud and slightly worried, like people who'd raised a brilliant but slightly unhinged child, who just happened to be thirty-two years old. They were either too scared to get involved or brave enough to leave him to it.

All the Clouet Champagnes were Blanc de Noirs, made purely from the famed Bouzy Pinot Noir. And they were remarkable – powerful yet refined, like liquid silk with bubbles. But it was JF himself who stole the show, as he presented each bottle to us along with its own elaborate story.

'Zis one,' he declared, holding up a bottle of his Brut Rosé, 'is like my grandmuzza – beautiful, elegant, but with a hidden strength zat could knock out a German soldier!' I wasn't entirely sure if he was joking.

One minute he was explaining the precise geological formation of Bouzy's chalk soils, the next he was pulling out what might have been his ancestor's sword, preparing to sabre his favourite bottle.

'Watch ziyss!' he announced. We were about to witness either grand theatre or catastrophe, possibly both.

I'd never seen this done before – sabrage – supposedly the elegant art of opening Champagne with one swift swipe of a blade. I'd heard it needs to be done with surgical precision, a gentle slide of the blade along the bottle's seam, giving a clean pop as the collar and cork fly off together. That's what I'd heard, anyway.

JF was no newcomer to this. With an air of steely menace, he approached the bottle as if challenging it to a duel.

'Now watch zis. Zis is how my great-grandfazza did it!' he

proclaimed, swinging the sabre violently, but with more gusto than accuracy. On his first attempt, he sent an antique crystal glass flying and missed the bottle altogether.

'Oh booooolsheet!' he declared.

His second swipe of the sabre landed with more accuracy – significantly more. The blade glided up the neck, clipped the top off beautifully and the cork and collar separated cleanly. But instead of a small plume of Champagne from the pressure, a geyser of biblical proportions gushed out, instantly drenching the wall, the ceiling and eventually me, in my smart blue shirt and, of course, the habitual cream chinos. I looked like I'd wet myself.

JF was bent double in stitches as I stood dripping with his finest Grand Cru Champagne, a maniacal grin plastered across his face.

'You see?' he beamed, 'Perfect! Just like my great-grandfazza do eet!'

His late great-grandfazza was probably spinning in his grave fast enough to make his own bubbles.

The wine, though (what was left in the severed bottle), was magnificent – that same brioche and red apples I'd first tasted back in London – and with not one piece of shattered glass. Moments later, JF's mother appeared, took one look at the scene and me in my wet chinos, and merely sighed the sigh of a woman who had seen this movie before.

'Next time,' the son announced, 'I show you how my grandfazza opened ze bottles in the dark during the occupation!' Madame Clouet's expression suggested this was one family tradition that might need to skip a generation.

By the time we left the Clouet residence that day, I wasn't sure if I'd just experienced a wine tasting or auditioned for an avant-garde French theatre production. What I did know was that I'd never look at Bouzy – or indeed, Champagne – the same way again. We'd found a truly fabulous new Champagne. Almost as fabulous, in fact, as the lunatic who made it.

And then, at the height of summer 2003, JF came to London to 'help' me make an impact at a dinner for 400 guests in the Natural History Museum. Picture this: that Victorian cathedral to nature where Dippy the Diplodocus has overseen more smart dinners than the Royal Family. JF was to be the guest of honour, presenting his Grand Cru Champagne to the distinguished guests from a balcony overlooking the great hall. What could possibly go wrong?

My first challenge was getting him there. I wasn't sure if JF had ever left France before, and extracting a Champagne grower from his vineyard is like trying to separate a bear from a beehive – possible, but needs some clever distraction. So, after our unforgettable visit to Bouzy, I decided it was safest to drive to France to collect him, convinced that if left to his own devices, he'd find a vine that needed an emergency pruning or maybe meet some beautiful lady en route and disappear to Holland.

I got him to London without incident and he stayed at our house the night before the event. London was melting in a heatwave; David Beckham was breaking our hearts heading to Madrid from Man United; they were filming *Love Actually* up the road in Notting Hill . . . and Beth was cooking a delicious *'très anglais'* supper with which I'd be serving some tasty non-French wine. Our twin daughters, Georgia and India, decided to provide their own unique brand of hospitality too. Aged four and wearing matching mischievous grins, they were tasked with the simple job of placing a jug of water by his bedside. Everything was going to be perfect for our new friend Jean-François.

The next morning, he appeared at breakfast, moving slightly slowly but remarkably cheerful.

'How did you sleep?' I asked.

'Oh, very well ssssank you. I am a bit tired, zoh,' he announced in his thick French accent. 'Zeyr seemed to be quite a lot of water in my bed.' The twins, it turned out, had interpreted put the jug of water 'by the bed' as 'in the bed', and had somehow emptied the entire jug between the sheets. With the precision of master sommeliers, they'd managed to create what JF later described as 'a perfect water terroir'.

But instead of throwing a very justified French fit, he declared it 'an authentic English welcome' and proceeded to tell the girls stories about how the vines in Champagne get water. Turns out he was more than just a winemaker; he was a diplomat, too. By breakfast's end, they were plotting to create their very own vineyard in their paddling pool.

That night, the National History Museum dinner was a perfect collision of French charm meeting British pomp. JF stood up on the balcony, his fabulously French voice echoing around Dippy's bones, and thanked the 400 diners for such a warm welcome to 'ze Natural Hysteria Museum' – which, given the circumstances of his wake-up call, seemed oddly appropriate.

He had them eating out of his hand – or, more accurately, drinking right out of his bottles – telling them stories about how his family had hidden their best wines from the Nazis. Even the Natural History Museum's director, who'd initially looked worried about having a rough and ready Frenchman gesticulating wildly above her precious dinosaur, would later ask him about vineyard visits.

That evening marked the beginning of a friendship that's grown like a vigorous vine. JF has gone on to become one of the most serious and well-respected winemakers in Champagne, the mayor of his Grand Cru town, Bouzy, and his bottles grace the tables of the Swedish royal family. 'In Bouzy, we don't make wine . . . we make liquid dreams!' he says.

Every time I open one of his bottles now, I think about that morning at our house in London – the look of bemused acceptance on his face, the twins' proud announcement that they'd 'helped John from Square' (as they pronounced his name) with his water, and the way he turned what could have been a disaster into the foundation of a beautiful friendship. He was, and actually is, the craziest, most eccentric winemaker I've ever met – utterly brilliant, and impossible not to love. And that applies to his wines, too.

Often wine gets a bad rep for stuffiness, a bit of a boring drink compared to colourful cocktails and characterful craft beers, so it helps to have characters like JF. In him I've met a supreme master of the stage. A creator with flare who brings his wines to life. But it's not just winemakers who bring wine to life, there are others too: the passionate merchants and of course the restaurant staff who really know their onions – the sommeliers.

The sommeliers, or 'somms' as some wine hipsters call them, are the men and women who decipher the restaurant wine list for us. While they can be the most intimidating people in the wine game, they can also be the making of your restaurant experience.

Thirty years ago, it seemed to me that they were all

black-clad wine ninjas who, when I nervously asked for a glass of Gewürztraminer, desperately trying to sound like I wasn't having a coughing fit, were simply there to make me feel like I should be back in short trousers. (To this day I still find it the most difficult grape variety to pronounce, but one I love. It's the wine I give to anybody who claims white wine just tastes of wine. This doesn't, it's a glass full of lychees, Turkish delight and rosewater, a bit like drinking a refreshing perfumery.) I digress though; back to those somms. I'm talking here about the type who can make the simple act of presenting a bottle feel like a West End production, complete with dramatic pauses and theatrical flourishes – my worst nightmare.

While I'd be flustering, red-faced, with their leather-bound tome of vinous treasures – to these guys a work of art in itself (and they did seem to be all guys back then) – I could sense them looking haughty, bored, and oh-so judgemental. It's as if they'd all attended special classes in Advanced Eyebrow Raising and Professional Sighing.

I remember an early encounter with a proper 'French' sommelier. A real Fawlty Towers moment. He slid up to my table like Count Dracula approaching my neck, his silver tastevin gleaming against his black jacket. (As the word suggests, a tastevin is an ornate silver wine-tasting cup worn on a chain (very rarely seen these days), to take just a sip of the wine.)

'Monsieur wishes to see the wine list?' he asked, his French accent polished probably in Plymouth rather than Bordeaux. I nodded, trying to look like this was a regular occurrence for me.

The list arrived – about the same size as the Oxford English Dictionary, bound in leather, probably sourced from cows raised on a diet of Château Lafite. He handed it to me with the reverence of a priest passing over sacred texts, then stood over my shoulder, waiting and watching. I was frantically flipping through the pages, searching for any safe name I knew or anything I could even pronounce, while feeling the beads of sweat forming on my brow. Sancerre . . . I pointed at a Sancerre, my finger trembling like I was diffusing a bomb.

'Yes, let's have a bottle of Domaine Gitton's Sancerre, please.' With, I think it was, a chicken terrine!!

The sommelier looked at me as if I'd just called his mother a slut but he waddled off to get the bottle, then went through the whole rigmarole of show, tell and pour. Then, and this is the bit that really drives me mad, he took the bottle away and never returned to top up our glasses! It was worthy of a Michael McIntyre prank.

In the world of fine dining, sommeliers have evolved into something far more than just wine stewards and custodians of the cellar; sometimes, sadly, with their carefully cultivated knowledge and precise palates, I can find them much scarier too. Hovering by my side, waiting for my wine choice, they can transform a planned relaxed, fun evening into a high-stakes performance. I can almost hear them say, 'Go on then, let's see what you've got,' as they test and scrutinise my wine knowledge.

I'm sure sommeliers don't try to be intimidating. It's just that they've spent so long studying so hard in a world that's invented much of its own language – the 'language of vinous exclusivity' – a tool that's actually a barrier with descriptives that mystify most of us.

Consider the moment when a sommelier approaches the table. 'Do you have any preferences in mind?' seems innocuous enough, yet it immediately imposes a subtle power dynamic. We've now got to reveal our limited wine knowledge by using general terms – 'red, white, anything under £40 . . .?' 'Maybe something full-bodied?' – or we're brave enough to get a bit more specific and risk being shown up . . . not that this would be the intention of any good sommelier.

The whole show of wine service piles on the intimidation. It's theatre I know, but I don't want to be one of the actors. The sommeliers' practised movements – the precise angle they hold the bottle, the measured pour, the expectant pause as they await your approval – they make pouring a drink into something akin to an elaborate ballet, a dance complicated with plenty of opportunities for social missteps. Should I swirl the wine? Smell it? Comment on its legs?

But these types shouldn't be allowed to give all sommeliers a bad rep. In fact, they shouldn't be allowed in a restaurant at all, because the good ones are good. In fact, they're absolutely brilliant. They're like the Special Forces of the restaurant world, capable of defusing wine-list panic with amiable aplomb. They can decode a table's undercurrents with just a few seemingly casual questions: who is trying to impress whom, who's paying, who's worried about looking a fool, then – much like a sabre to a Champagne bottle – with clinical precision they begin unveiling their recommendations from their treasure chest wine list.

I remember once in a restaurant in Glasgow a sommelier who, after watching me struggle with the list for approximately three seconds, in a strong Glaswegian accent said simply, 'Tell me about the last wine that made you happy.' No pretention, no judgement, just genuine interest. We ended up discussing obscure Austrian Zweigelts while the three friends I was eating with began to panic that they were never going to get a drink.

The really good sommeliers are like wine whisperers – able to read a table better than a poker player. They know instantly whether you're a wine geek like me wanting to nerd out, or a nervous novice needing guidance, or someone who just wants a decent glass of red sharpish. I've witnessed a sommelier talk a table of rowdy city boys down from a 'top of the list' Bordeaux to a Super (but not *that* super) Tuscan red at half the price . . . and they loved it. That's not just good service – that's proper salesmanship.

They also have this remarkable ability to materialise exactly when needed and vanish when you're having an intimate moment with your glass . . . But, unlike that 'French' chap way back when, they'll remember to return and refill it. It's like they've mastered an enigmatic superpower of vinous teleportation. The truly great ones can even predict what you want before you know it yourself, appearing with a decanter just as you're about to mention that the wine might need to breathe.

Yes, the restaurant world and sommeliers who work within it have come a long, long way in my experience. It's taken a while and, in my humble opinion, we're not there quite yet, but I'll always ask the sommelier for a recommendation if the list looks like it's been constructed well and it seems like it could be an adventure for me. My joy is to discover something new and delicious and when I do, I leave the restaurant very happy. What's more I'll have made another wine friend and I'll be sure to go back . . . when I can next afford it.

Worst sommelier moment? I'll tell you. It was while I was studying the Master of Wine programme, one evening, perched at the bar of one of London's swankiest establishments with three clients who'd become, and are still now, great friends. It sort of happens in the wine game. Along came the sommelier and we recognised each other. We were both studying for the same section of the MW course so I asked him to recommend a 'freshen-up' wine before we sat for dinner. Being a good wine geek and a well-trained sommelier – the type who knows they can recommend a wine that cost more than my first car and get away with it – he went for a Riesling from JJ Prüm, one of the best growers of the great, slaty, mineral-packed German white. I was looking forward to this.

And off he went, pouring all four glasses without offering me a taste – a little bit like, I'd imagine, a skydiving instructor pushing you out of the plane without having done the parachute safety check. Not the kind of service you expect in such an upmarket establishment.

My guests were wine enthusiasts – i.e., they loved a glass of wine but didn't know too much about it – and so they got stuck in, while my 'friend' Herr Sommelier, who *was* in fact German, nailed me to the floor with facts on the geological history of the Mosel. And this was only the opening gambit in what I soon realised was a good old-fashioned dick-swinging contest.

My friends, meanwhile, were sipping and nodding sagely. One had the 'wine face' on – that thoughtful expression people pull when they're looking for the magic that I was surely going to point out to them as soon as I got rid of Herr Sommelier and could join them. The other was staring into his glass like it was a crystal ball and 'getting notes of . . . wine?'

And, when at last my German sommelier friend got distracted by another customer, it was my turn to taste the Riesling. They passed me my glass and the aroma hit me before the glass got anywhere near my nose. That unmistakable smell of wet cardboard and crushed dreams – cork taint, or 2,4,6-trichloroanisole to give it its real name (TCA), the killer for all good wine. It was so corked it was worthy of a place in the Museum of Wine Faults.

'I'm terribly sorry,' I told the sommelier, in my most diplomatic tone possible, 'I think this is corked. Can you have a taste?'

My guests breathed noticeable sighs of relief. Their shoulders dropped and they relaxed as I explained to them that JJ Prüm is the master of Mosel Riesling and he doesn't make wine that smells of a bus shelter.

'I have,' the sommelier replied looking very smug and very pleased with himself. 'It's his Wehlener Sonnenuhr, a very complex wine [read . . . too complex for *me*] and it's the spices coming through.'

'Spppiiices,' I thought to myself. 'I'll show you spppiiices!!' I nearly spat my two front teeth out, I was so cross.

Suddenly, my three friends had front-row seats for a big boss sommelier/T. Gilbey stand-off. One was pretending to read the menu upside down, the other was checking out his shoelaces, and the third appeared to be moments away from jumping into a taxi.

'Could you taste it again, please,' I asked, desperately trying to keep control of myself but really wanting to take a hay-baler swing at him across the bar.

'I opened it myself,' he responded.

'It's getting even better,' I thought to myself. A proper trainwreck, only in slow motion. My blood pressure was rising but somehow I managed to control myself and order a fresh bottle of something that *I* was going to choose and that *I* was going to taste before he went ahead and poured anybody else's glass. It's not that I'm precious but wine is my thing and I'm not going to sit there silently and watch my three friends drink 'off' wine when I know it's off. That's a big fat NO.

But there's not much that I've enjoyed more than getting a really good win in a restaurant and I'm not talking about just getting a great bottle or glass of wine. I'm talking about winning the jackpot as I did once in 1997.

I was twenty-five, I'd just taken the job with Jack Scott and was full of that dangerous combination of a bit of wine knowledge and a lot of youthful bravado, and I'd taken Beth to dinner at Rick Stein's Seafood Restaurant in Padstow, Cornwall. I knew the restaurant well, as it was the place Mum and Dad treated themselves and their guests to on their annual trip to Cornwall. It was everything I'd imagined a fancy restaurant to be – starched white tablecloths, more forks than the average person has fingers, waiting staff all smartly uniformed, and a sommelier who looked like he'd been decanting wines since before the French Revolution. It was, and is, one of my favourite restaurants anywhere on earth, and it was proper treat time.

I'd borrowed Mum's knackered old Volvo 360 for the week and it now sat in the harbour car park across the road, innocently unaware it was about to become the getaway car for what I still consider to be one of my greatest ever (legal) wine heists.

I flicked through the wine list, skipping over Burgundy, Bordeaux and all the other regions that were far too pricy for any regular twenty-something. I headed to Alsace – then and still a much underrated and underpriced region for stunning white wines, some of which, the dry Rieslings and Pinot Blancs, are just perfect with Rick's menu. And there it was, one of my favourites, the Riesling by Maison Trimbach. It's still a go-to for me today – deliciously fresh when young, with lime, lemon and a whiff of a summer meadow. So, when the sommelier eventually arrived and, having calculated that I could still stretch to coffee after dinner, I went for it.

'An excellent choice,' was the response. So far so good, and off he scurried. Though goodness knows where, he was gone for a while. He'd have been back quicker if he'd gone over to Alsace and got the bottle from the vineyard himself but return he eventually did, halfway through our starter, to proudly reveal the chilled bottle of Riesling. But it wasn't the ordinary Riesling by Trimbach at all, it was the all-singing, all-dancing Cuvée Frédéric Emile version, named after one of the famous Trimbach ancestors and the blend of two of the best Grand Cru vineyards in Alsace. This, I knew, was everything I could expect from the Riesling I'd actually ordered... but much, much more. *This* Riesling was turbocharged and should have been about three times the price of the bottle I ordered... more like £50 a bottle at least.

For those of you who remember what it's like to pay for things in cash, well, you'll probably also remember those happy moments when the check-out cashier gives you too much change, or when a waiter hands you the bill in a restaurant and they've forgotten to charge for the cocktails. Do you tell them or do you dash?

On this occasion, I'm proud to say that I played fair.

'This isn't the one I ordered,' I said. 'This is the Cuvée Frédéric Emile.'

'Well, it's the only Riesling we have, sir,' the ancient sommelier replied, and when he offered it to me at the same price as the wine I'd originally ordered, my mind went into overdrive...

'Do you have any more of this you'd be happy to sell me at this price?' I asked, trying to sound nonchalant and trying also not to create yet another situation where Beth wants to leave the restaurant before she's finished the starter.

'I think we have seventeen bottles,' he replied, thinking, I'm sure, that I was planning a two-bottle dinner, and wanted to stick on the same juice throughout.

'You know, it's very underpriced,' I proffered, 'but if you're happy with it, can I please buy them all and you add them to the bill?'

Suddenly we'd become the main act for the two tables either side of us. Beth did now want to get up and leave. She hadn't yet eaten her scallops and the sommelier looked at me as if I was a lunatic they'd let out on day release.

'All... seventeen?' he spluttered.

'Yes, please. We'll drink this one with dinner and put the others in the car outside.'

'I don't see why not,' came the answer and, just like that, sixteen bottles of Riesling Cuvée Frédéric Emile became the backbone of my humble wine collection.

And, sweet mercy, when I tasted it for the first time that night, it was glorious – all lime blossom and wet stones, with an acidity that could strip paint, yet somehow it remained as elegant as Grace Kelly at a state banquet.

This really was turbocharged and it took a good, firm kick under the table from Beth to get me to start eating my starter again and talk about anything other than planning a holiday to Alsace.

The fun came again after we'd finished our quite superb meal (thank you, Rick!). Now we had the logistical challenge of leaving the restaurant with two cases of wine and a growing audience of amused kitchen staff who'd gathered to watch the lunatic pay and leave. But the sommelier and I were now firm friends and he helped us pack the car like we were playing the world's most expensive game of Tetris. All sixteen bottles, carefully wrapped in tissue paper, nestled into the back of Mum's beaten-up Volvo like sleeping babies.

The drive home was an exercise in paranoia. Mum's antique Volvo 360 struggled with Cornwall's hills as it was, so slamming a couple of cases of fine Alsatian dry white in the boot was really testing its Swedish-built mettle. Beth went silent with rage, I think, and every bump, every corner, brought a gentle tinkle of glass on glass that sent shivers down my spine. She'd only had one glass of the Riesling, and she drove slower than a nonagenarian on a mobility scooter, but we made it. What's more, all these years later, whenever I see or, even better, taste Cuvée Frédéric Emile, I am transported back to that evening – the look on the sommelier's face dealing with this jumped-up pup and Beth's desperate expression as I went into delirious excitement. It is still one of my 'go-to' favourite wines – expensive now but just as impressive as it's ever been.

And somewhere in Padstow, I like to think there's still a sommelier or two who'd make it into the annals of another young, keen wino, by doing the same for him or her.

HOW TO CHOOSE WINE IN A RESTAURANT

- Don't panic when the waiter/sommelier/maître d' hands you the wine list – I like to set out my stall early by telling them I'd like a little guidance. I then say I need a few minutes alone with the list, then could they come back and help me choose.

- Trust the house wine – good restaurants take pride in their house selection. They've chosen it to reflect their standards and it's often fantastic value.

- Stick to your budget, not what you think the sommelier would like you to spend – you can have great wine experiences at every price point. Set your budget and don't waver; the sommelier will respect that.

- Use the sommelier's expertise – they love their list and know where the real value lies. Tell them what you usually enjoy and your price range. They're there to help, not judge.

- Consider the food – but don't get too hung up on perfect pairings. Think weight and intensity rather than any rigid rules. A light dish wants a lighter wine and vice versa.

- Start light – especially if ordering multiple bottles. Then you can move on to the heavier wines. Your palate will thank you.

- Check the vintage and don't just assume that older is always better – it isn't. Age can bring complexity to fine wines but can tire out simpler ones.

- Look for the hidden gems – seek out second labels from famous producers, lesser-known regions similar to famous ones (think Crozes-Hermitage instead of Hermitage), or unfashionable vintages, which all can offer brilliant value.

- Think about the occasion – a celebration calls for something different from a casual Tuesday dinner. Let the moment guide you as much as the food.

- Be confident and have fun – pronounce the name of the wine however you like. Remember: nobody else in the restaurant knows what they're doing either and wine is ultimately about pleasure. If you enjoy it, you've chosen well.

Wine Wanker Approved List #6:
Ten Favourite Sparkling Wines

(**Hero bottle** – *Champagne André Clouet Cuvée 1911*)

Laurent-Perrier Grande Siècle, Tours-sur-Marne, France
Drink this and you'll realise how great Champagne really can be. It's Laurent-Perrier's prestige cuvée – so rich and complex. People often talk of the brioche and toasty notes you get in the best Champagnes, well, you'll find those in this wine, which is right up there with the best of the best from the region.

Camel Valley Rosé Brut, Bodmin, Cornwall, England
I can't get enough of this sparkling pink. It's like liquidised, sparkling strawberries. Everybody I serve it to prefers it to rosé Champagne or Prosecco and, in fact, I love it so much we served it at my son and daughter-in-law's (Fred and Shekhinah) wedding in Cornwall.

Champagne André Clouet Grand Cru 'Blanc de Noirs' Champagne, Bouzy, France
I know the hero bottle for this chapter is André Clouet's Prestige Cuvée 1911, but I completely love this wine, their regular NV Brut. It doesn't cost the earth; it looks more beautiful than any bottle and label I've ever seen and the sparkles inside are head-spinningly delicious. In short – total class.

Léonce Bocquet Crémant de Bourgogne, Burgundy, France
I'm a massive fan of sparkling wines made outside Champagne but using the same Champagne method, and of these, Crémant is what to look out for. Eight regions are allowed

to produce it in France, and this one from Burgundy is gorgeously fresh and creamy, just as good as many Champagnes I've tried.

Ayala Le Blanc de Blancs Champagne, Aÿ, France
No, it's not the most expensive, nor the flashiest of Champagnes . . . because, it's Ayala and they focus on making great fizz rather than sponsoring James Bond and/or posh polo matches. In fact, they make one of my favourite Blanc de Blancs Champagnes – all lemons and biscuits with a waft of the old bakery to it too. Try a magnum of it for twice the fun.

Cloudy Bay Pelorus, Marlborough, New Zealand
This is one of my favourite sparklers from outside Europe. I first tried it at Chez Bruce restaurant in Wandsworth in 1998 and got a bit wobbly with it because it was soooo delicious. It's crisp but carries a bit of weight to it. It's very, very good and quite affordable, too.

Ruinart Blanc de Blancs NV Champagne, Reims, France
Ruinart is the oldest Champagne house on record and this is my favourite of their wines; in fact, it's my favourite Champagne. It's made with 100 per cent Chardonnay and I'd describe it as a tart's Champagne (of which I am certainly one btw) – all bright citrus fruit. When I'm with my Northern Irish friend Brendan we drink it from large wine glasses with plenty of ice and it's totally . . . *delicious.*

Louis Roederer Quartet NV Brut, Anderson Valley, California, USA
This is the Champagne company Louis Roederer's project in California and it's an excellent value, completely delicious sparkler. A blend of Pinot Noir and Chardonnay, it's full of delicious orchard-like fruit. Dry and very, very tasty.

Nyetimber Blanc de Blancs, West Sussex, England
My favourite UK sparkler and the pioneers of Chardonnay and the Pinots for English sparkling wine. It balances citrus-like crisp acidity with delicious richness. It's an incredible glass of fizz.

Pol Roger 'Cuvée Sir Winston Churchill', Champagne, France
The flagship wine of this great estate and it's like a bakery meets a fruit shop, meets a florist. Incredibly complex and totally seductive. It's one of my absolute favourites if I ever get the chance to try it.

7
Good Shit

CHATEAU MARIS
2009
LA TOUGE SYRAH

Hero bottle: *Château Maris 'La Touge' Syrah, Minervois-La-Livinière*

'Smell that,' Bertie instructed me, as he pulled his fist out of a large pile of steaming manure and shoved it in my face. May 2004 and we were standing at the front gates of his property – Château Maris in the Minervois, between Toulouse and Montpellier in the Languedoc region of southern France.

'What's that?' he asked.

'It's shit,' I replied.

'No, Tom,' he wagged his free finger at me. 'It's *good* shit. Come with me.'

And so we walked through the vines and up the hill to get a viewpoint of the entire thirty-two-hectare estate.

After thirty years in the wine business, my biggest lesson has been that you don't really get to understand a wine unless you understand where it comes from. All the really useful experience and knowledge I've gained has come from my field trips, as I like to call them, spending time out in the vineyards and wineries, and not so much from the classroom, or the tasting room. Yes, the analytical stuff is important, but for me, it's more about the emotion – how a wine makes me feel. And, if it tastes sublime and I have a connection with it, it will make me feel great. This field trip to Château Maris and tasting Bertie's wine was to waken some very different emotions in me, for reasons that will become apparent. But for starters, I felt wonder and admiration. It opened my eyes to a whole new way of growing vines and winemaking.

'Where are the borders of my vineyards, Tom? Point them out to me,' Bertie said as we continued our walk.

This was a fun game. Believe it or not, it was also my work – I was being paid to walk around beautiful vineyards playing I spy with this infectiously enthusiastic nutcase, Robert 'Bertie' Eden. He'd bought the Château Maris vineyards in 1997 and I knew that from the outset he had followed organic farming principles and that he'd been growing his wine biodynamically since 2002. But I had never knowingly tasted a biodynamic wine before. As far as I was aware, this was also the first time I'd set foot on a biodynamic estate. And what I was seeing was absolutely incredible.

Bertie's vineyards were bordered on two sides by non-organic vineyards and the distinction was like night and day. Bertie's vines looked magnificent, vigorous with bushy green foliage and dark, thick, strong muscular trunks and stems. By contrast, the neighbouring vines on both sides looked sick and knackered – positively wimpy with far fewer leaves and more brown in colour.

I was witnessing the changing tide of the Languedoc-Roussillon, an area that was referred to as the toilet of wine production, reviled for producing some of the most average wine in circulation at the time, made by growers who for years had been subsidised to produce more and more wine that ended up in the infamous 'wine lake of Europe'.

By 2004, wine growers were being paid to grub up their vines, so much of what I was looking at from my vista point was wasteland – battered and bruised-looking fields with no vines on at all. They'd taken the EU subsidy and done the right thing.

At Château Maris, however, Bertie had gone the other way. He understood that the conditions in the Minervois, particularly where he was, near the village of La Livinière, were ideal for growing the Syrah grape – plenty of sunshine, not too much rain and a bit of a breeze every now and then, to boot. These are the perfect conditions for avoiding disease, so in he'd plunged to the business of winemaking. But he was doing things a little differently, devoted to following a sustainable environmental and regenerative ideal. The first priority was to restore the natural fertility of the badly depleted soil – giving back and replenishing rather than always taking. The winery itself was also founded on these sustainable and carbon-neutral principles – Bertie used gravity wherever possible to move the wine through the winemaking process and was building his cellar, which sat beside an ancient Visigothic chapel, with thick hemp walls and covered with a 'living' green roof. Within eight years he would have established one of most environmentally friendly wineries in the world. I had never met anybody like this before. But, of course, thought I, it's all very well to have healthy land and vines and to be doing all these impressive things in and around the wine estate, but if the Château Maris wine is no good, what's the point?

So, into the tasting room we went, and well, there I discovered one of *the* stand-out spectacular wines of my life. Bertie must have poured me half-a-dozen different wines, all either organic or biodynamic, and they were all really tasty but then I took a sniff of this one, his Château Maris 'La Touge' Syrah 2002. Made 100 per cent biodynamically, dark inky black, it had an energy about it and an intensity that surpassed everything else on the tasting table. I could smell it from three feet away, jumping out of the glass with ripe blackcurrant and blackberry fruit. I could smell other things too – hints of cream, vanilla and cinnamon – all wrapped up in the Syrah's juicy envelope of fruit. And then I tasted it – the darkest, softest velvet gliding across my tongue. It warmed my throat reminding me that it was, under its elegant guise, a 14.5 per cent ABV bruiser that wasn't to be trifled with. It was absolutely bleedin' delicious and, what's more, it wasn't the most expensive wine on the table, just €4 excluding tax if we were to import it, but it was the most beautifully balanced wine, and one that I come back to again and again today.

Now, I've come across my fair share of scepticism about biodynamic wine. And out and about in this world of wine, the moment I hear anyone mention the practice of burying cow horns filled with manure in among the vines under a full moon, I see how most other people start throwing a few weird looks at each other. But I've seen it first hand – Bertie Eden's prize-fighter vines flourishing next to their sickly conventionally grown neighbours. I'm a true believer and I hope you'll humour me in setting this in a bit of context . . .

Organic wine is all about farming without industrial synthetic pesticides, herbicides and fertilisers. Grown this way the vines rely on natural defences, good old-fashioned compost, and the farmer's attention rather than chemicals. The result? Healthier soil, happier ecosystems, and hopefully happier, tastier wines . . . But not all the time.

Biodynamic farming, on the other hand, is like the mystical older sibling of the organic movement. The concept of biodynamic growing was developed in the 1920s by Rudolf Steiner, a highly regarded Austrian scientist and philosopher, as a method of farming that follows the cosmos – in other words, each stage of the sowing, growing and harvesting cycle is plotted according to lunar cycles and planetary positions. It's the other ritual aspects and weird preparations, though, that raise eyebrows the most. Those cow horns I mentioned earlier really are packed with manure, buried over winter, dug up in spring, and the contents are then diluted and sprayed on the vines to fight disease. And if it's not manure, it's horn silica (ground quartz), also packed into the cow horns and buried over summer. Or they're packing yarrow flowers into stag bladders to ferment; chamomile fermenting in deer intestines. Yes, I know, it sounds mad and totally 'out there' and it still seems so to me, like something from a medieval apothecary rather than modern agriculture – until you actually see the results, as I did for the first time that day at Château Maris.

The modern biodynamic farm is increasingly a self-sustaining ecosystem. Walking through Bertie's vineyard that May day in 2004, it wasn't the prettiest, most manicured I've seen, but between the rows grew a host of diverse herbs and flowers, attracting all sorts of beneficial insects and natural predators keeping pests in check. And the soil beneath my feet wasn't just dry, dusty dirt – it was alive, teeming with worms and microorganisms. I could smell it, soil with that rich, earthy vitality Bertie had thrust into my face moments previously. Then, standing there among the thriving vines, another penny dropped for me.

'My wine is made in the vineyard, Tom. Everything else is just careful observation,' Bertie told me . . . and I'm still with him on that. Whether it's organic or full biodynamic moon-calendar crazy, the wine's just that extra bit special to me.

Over the years, I've now visited many more organic-biodynamic wineries, and their vines are stronger, healthier and surely more resistant to disease than their chemical-dependent neighbours. But, as I said, ultimately it's all about the wines and that's where you really *can* taste the difference. The biodynamic wines I've tasted seem to have an energy about them, a vibrancy that's very hard to explain. (Really, the best thing would be to shut this book, buy a trusted biodynamic bottle, and take a sip right now.) But let's just say they have something extra, a brightness, a clarity of flavour, that sets them apart, almost like they're telling you a story through taste. It's a bit like listening to an author narrate their book, rather than reading it for yourself.

Both organic and biodynamic winemaking is a serious business. To gain organic certification a winery must prove at least three years of chemical-free farming; for a biodynamic (usually Demeter) certification, you need first to have gained an organic certification plus proof of adherence to the biodynamic calendar and preparations. It's not just about what you *don't* do – use of industrial chemicals, etc., etc. – it's about what you actively *do* do in order to enhance the life of the vineyard. A biodynamic wine estate will have set aside a whole area to prepare and store all the magical potions used to maintain the healthy vineyard, and to visit here is to walk into the most sensual perfumery you can imagine. I've seen it and smelt it at Château Climens in Sauternes to the south of Bordeaux, which is famed for its incredible and fabulously expensive sweet wines. And there the charmingly rustic drying room is fragrant with camomile and many other natural plants, all ready for the preparations.

By the time I saw the Château Maris biodynamic

revolution, I'd been in the London wine trade for nearly a decade, spending a lot of my life pinging between the major producing areas of France, Italy and Spain. Sometimes my excitement was from experiencing and seeing new growing and winemaking methods. Sometimes from visiting new regions and discovering new landscapes. But it wasn't until I went on a journey to South Africa in 2008 that I experienced such jaw-hits-the-floor natural beauty.

Beth and our extended family had booked a 'once in a lifetime' holiday for her dad's eightieth birthday. The trip began with a safari and ended in Cape Town. Of course, this was an unmissable opportunity so I'd wangled it with Jack to tag on an extra week's stay. I would visit winegrowers in the Cape, some of whom we dealt with already and some we wanted to deal with. So, I waved Beth and our four children goodbye at the airport and hit the road to Stellenbosch in my hire car – unfortunately with no satnav... just an old-school roadmap and my suitcase.

Driving into the Cape winelands, you'll be confronted with one of the most beautiful wine-growing regions you will ever see. Here the mighty Franschhoek Mountains tower like ancient guardians over valleys carpeted with vines, each row marching with military precision towards an impossibly blue horizon. It was exhilarating. Whooping with joy, I rolled down all the car windows and stuck my head out. Outside the air was thick with possibility, wildflowers and fertile earth promising untold numbers of unknown wines that I was yet to discover.

Pressing on along the Stellenbosch wine route, I drove through the area's small towns, their old Dutch architecture sitting proudly against that vast African sky, white-washed walls gleaming like pearls in the morning light. I could sense the centuries of winemaking history here; there was a special energy that enthralled me – maybe it was knowing that perhaps my great-great-great-grandfather Alfred and his brother Walter had gone here before me, that this land was the original source of their winemaking empire. But it wasn't about history – this wasn't some dusty museum of viticulture: it was a living, breathing wine paradise finding its voice, and I wanted to do whatever I could to lend a helping hand.

I kept driving past signs advertising wine sales, tastings and free tours and I couldn't resist taking a short unplanned detour to Cavalli Wine Estate. I had to taste a Chenin Blanc – and it was a showstopper. Actually, there in the vineyard, the morning sun warming my glass, it was like discovering wine all over again. With a vibrancy that captured the very essence of these soils, these slopes, this light, this Chenin proudly shouted out the story of its terroir to me. Standing there, looking out over that patchwork of vines, I knew I was experiencing one of those moments that would stay with me forever, filed away in that messy cabinet of wine memories I carry around in my head.

But I had to remind myself that I was there on a buying trip, hunting bargains. The exchange rate was favourable – eleven rand to the pound – so this had to be an opportunity to start filling up the top half of our restaurant customers' wine lists. Surely I could replace a few French Sauvignons and Merlots with South African alternatives and save a few quid. But, oh no . . . the Cape winegrowers, as wise as their ancient vines, had cottoned on long ago and quoted prices only in US dollars or sterling. And with my English accent, I felt like I was bartering in a Moroccan souk having rocked up in a Bentley and alighted wearing a tailcoat. But, bargain or no bargain, that didn't stop me tasting some exceptional wines on my way.

At the Simonsig Family Vineyards, their Cap Classique tap-danced on my tongue. It was like Krug's cheekier cousin – all that buttery sweet brioche and apple brightness at half the price. At the Thelema Mountain Vineyards, part of the spectacular Simonsberg mountain range, the Cabernet had me writing poetry in my tasting book – something about liquid velvet and cassis dreams, I think, though I'll never know. In all my excitement, I left that notebook behind in the tasting room.

At the historic 1797 Rickety Bridge Estate in the Franschhoek Valley, their Chenin Blanc tasted like honeysuckle had eloped with a lemon and run away to a spice market. We'd been selling it for a year or so, but tasting it here, with that panorama spreading out before me like God's own vineyard map, it was an entirely different beast. Nearby, lying in a vast and staggeringly beautiful valley basin between the Simonsberg and Drakenstein mountains, Boschendal Estate's Sauvignon Blanc tasted just as pretty as its label suggested – like drinking a fresh blade of grass dipped in tropical fruit juice. Sitting with one of their picnic hampers, looking out across the vines, was proof that you didn't need a smart table, or even any cutlery to have a memorable wine moment in this country.

Then, up I drove through the Franschhoek Pass, a hair-raising experience which all but killed me – hairpin bends that would give a mountain goat vertigo, drops steep enough to instantly age a wine. Next, it was into the Robertson valley, and to Arabella Wines, another old family winery, where fairytale Arabian horses pranced between the vines – it was like something from a wine-label designer's fever dream. Stephen and his son Jamie de Wet were now running the show here – the horses, the wine and the fruit growing – all achieved with a casual elegance that made me want to pack up the family home in London and move us all to the Cape. I mean, how bad of a commute could it be?!

This is where I had come to find value. Not the fancy pants wines of Stellenbosch and Franschhoek – I sought the honest, hardworking bottles that got the job done, that didn't need to show off and here, at Arabella, I found them. This was wine with dirt under its fingernails and sunshine in its soul. It made me realise I needed more.

After my decade in London's wine scene, buying and selling all sorts of (mainly European) wines, this trip to the Cape wineland felt different. I was feeding my soul here. I might not have been learning much about organics and biodynamics, but I was gorging on new wines, sunshine, history and the people. I was meeting characters who talked about terroir like others talk about their children, and who could read a grapevine like I read a wine list. It made me thirsty – not just for more wine, but for knowledge too. Real, proper, chuck-out-the-textbook-type knowledge, more understanding, more travel, if I was to properly have wine as part of my life.

As it happens, having arrived back in London, for my next adventure I didn't actually have to travel that far at all: across the Channel to Saumur in the Loire, in fact. It was around the time of the Angers wine fair, and I was going to see Xavier Amirault; little did I know it, but I was going to learn about a completely new way of making wine – the natural way.

When I arrived, the first thing I saw ... was him – a wild-haired man sporting a massive smile and a pair of traffic-cone-orange glasses like something out of Elton John's latest garage sale. His fingernails were black with soil and his T-shirt had more wine splatters than a Pollock. Here was my guide to the world of natural wine.

Out we walked into Xavier's vineyard.

'*Rien sulfeeetes*!' he announced proudly, arms spread wide like a circus conductor introducing his main act. 'Just grapes and gravity!'

I nodded politely while secretly working out how many cases of good old Chilean Cabernet I could be selling back home had I not been here being given a lesson in what I thought I already knew.

Then came my déjà vu. Xavier dropped to his knees and plunged his hands into the soil like a prospector panning for gold.

'Look!' he exclaimed, his orange glasses slipping down his nose as he scooped up a handful of earth teeming with worms and beetles. 'This is alive! Not like the dead dirt in chemical vineyards!'

'Christ!' I thought. 'Here we go again.'

And then, yes he did, he thrust the writhing handful of worms into my face.

Next he wanted to show me his cellar – but no déjà vu here. It was like nothing I'd seen before – no gleaming stainless-steel tanks, no neat rows of brand-new oak barrels. Instead, a collection of ancient oak *demi-muids* (500-litre barrels), concrete vats and vast clay amphorae stood like sleeping giants. The temperature dropped rapidly as we descended, and the earthy tang of wine hit my nostrils. It was a familiar smell but there was a whiff of something else too – something wild and untamed.

Xavier plunged a glass pipette into what looked like one of my O-level Chemistry experiments. The deep purple juice that emerged, all Cabernet Franc, was literally alive. He poured this into a glass where it now glistened in the dim cellar light.

'*Goûtez!*' Xavier commanded. And I did. The wine danced on my tongue with an energy I'd never before experienced, all vibrant fruit and that gorgeously chewy Loire freshness, but with something extra – an electric vitality that made my pedestrian tasting notes seem even less adequate than usual. So unfamiliar was the sensation of tasting Xavier's Cabernet Franc that I still find it hard to describe.

Now Xavier was bouncing around his cellar like a pinball, orange glasses a-flashing, drawing samples from various old oak barrels and vessels. Each wine told a different story – some weird, some wonderful, some just downright hideous, but all utterly unique. One smelled like fresh strawberries and wet stones; one of a horse's rear end; and another like wild herbs and summer rain.

'This is wine *sans maquillage*,' he declared, gesturing with a glass of something that glowed ruby red in the cellar light. 'No makeup. Natural beauty!' he grinned, revealing his purple-stained gnashers from his decades of tasting. And yet again, that penny dropped further. I was having another new wine experience.

By the sixth or seventh wine (who was counting?), my neat categories of what wine should be had started to blur. These weren't flawed wines – or well, they might have been to the Aussie winemakers of the nineties – instead they were wines with personality. Wines that reflected not just their terroir but the passionate lunatic who made them.

When we tried his top cuvée, Saint Nicolas de Bourgueil 'Le Fondis', a deep red wine made from Cabernet Franc, the classic red grape from the Loire, I finally and fully got the point. It had spent two years in a clay amphora and was like liquid silk woven from wild berries and crushed rocks. As Xavier waffled on about lunar cycles and cosmic energy, his Day-Glo orange specs appearing brighter and brighter the more excited he got, I found myself nodding along.

I said a fond goodbye to Xavier, leaving him with a large order for wines I'd have to work hard to sell back home, and me with a head full of questions. This eccentric, passionate genius in his Orangina eyewear had just thoroughly shaken up my neat little wine categories. But maybe I'd needed someone quirky to show me true sanity. Xavier and his natural wines had done exactly that.

If you'd told me thirty years ago that I'd be writing a book and in it I'd be raving about wines made in clay pots with grapes soaking with their skins like they're having a month-long spa treatment, I'd have thought you'd been at the cooking sherry. But here we go, and, although it took a while, these weird and wonderful wines have wormed their way into my heart.

So, what even is natural wine? Well, unlike biodynamic or organic wines, there are no defined parameters or official certifications, as such, but basically it's winemaking as nature intended, or at least as nature intended before we bollocksed it all up with 'clever' chemicals and fancy-pants equipment. In other words, no additives, few to no sulphites, no technological wizardry – just grapes doing their thing with minimal human interference.

The resulting wines can be anything from fabulous, interesting to literally undrinkable. I've drunk some that tasted like liquid sunshine filtered through a lavender garden; others more like they've been siphoned straight out of the River Thames. Some are more like homemade scrumpy than wine: cloudy and funky, with flavours that swing from barnyard to tropical fruit punch. Others are so pure and precise they scream their provenance from the rooftops. That's the same with any wine though; you can get good and bad of all sorts. But at their best, natural wines tend to have this incredible and inimitable vitality, exuding an elusive energy that makes conventional wines seem like they're still wearing a suit, stiff collar and tie.

Then there are the 'orange' wines. These are yet another level. These are natural wines made from white (or green) grapes but made like a red wine, where the grape skins stay in contact with the juice during fermentation. Although orange wines may seem like the bright new things on the block, in fact they're ancient history in a glass – they've been making wine this way in Georgia for 8,000 years. That's the fascinating thing about orange wines and natural wines as a category – they're simultaneously ancient and trendy. These methods – natural fermentation, skin contact, ageing in clay – are how everyone made wine before we got too clever for our own good. It's a bit like me discovering Dad's old collection of flared trousers and realising that once upon a time he properly rocked it.

The first time I tasted orange wine was a bit like Dorothy stepping into Oz, when the world goes from black and white to Technicolor. It was Georgian wine, aged in *qvevri* (large clay pots), and it hit me with flavours I didn't even have words for – honey and tea leaves, dried apricots and something that reminded me of walking through an autumn forest. There was also tannin, tangy nectarine, all sorts. As I tasted, it started out like a white wine, shifting to red wine territory, and finished somewhere in outer space. I'm not even sure if I liked it but suddenly I had to throw everything I thought I knew about wine out the window. It was time to start again.

The funny thing is, after years of studying wine, after all those exams (and I have done a few), all those hours of tastings and carefully scribbled notes, these wines came along and taught me that maybe we'd been taking it all a bit too seriously. These are the punk rockers of the wine world, throwing out the rulebook and shouting, 'Hey suckas! Wine doesn't need to wear a dinner jacket all of the time!'

Sure, these natural and orange wines aren't for everyone, and that's fine, but when they're good, believe me, they're something else. Try them instead of a pale crisp rosé from the south of France, as I did not long ago, and you'll be looking at the ceiling trying to work out if and why it works. It did for me. I tasted an orange wine with a beautifully barbecued *côte de boeuf* the other day – a bit of meat that screams 'give me a rich, robust red' – and it worked a treat. It was absolutely delicious with it. These wines remind me in fact of why us humans started making wine in the first place. They're alive, they're exciting, they tell stories.

TEN-STEP CHEAT-SHEET ON NATURAL VS ORGANIC AND BIODYNAMIC WINES

1. **THE BASIC PRINCIPLE** – while organic and biodynamic winegrowing focuses mainly on vineyard practices, natural wine is about the *whole* process – vineyard to bottle with minimal intervention. Nothing added, nothing taken away.

2. **EVERYTHING** in the natural wine vineyard must be at least organic (using no chemicals), but no organic certification is needed. Many natural winegrowers are also biodynamic, but again, no certification required. It's more about the philosophy than the paperwork.

3. **FERMENTATION** in natural wines uses only wild yeasts – those that are naturally present on grape skins or in the winery. Organic and biodynamic winegrowers often do the same but they may still use commercial yeasts.

4. **THE SULPHUR STORY.** Natural wines have little or no added sulphites (organic certification allows up to 100ppm, conventional up to 200ppm). Natural wines typically have under 30ppm, and often zero.

5. **THE LOOK.** Natural wines are usually unrefined and unfiltered – they can appear cloudy, sometimes with visible sediment. Organic and biodynamic wines are typically clear.

6. **THE TASTE.** Some argue that natural wines taste more 'alive' – funky, fresh and unpredictable. They sometimes can taste more like cider than conventional wine and, because they're generally less stable than traditional wines, they're more variable bottle to bottle.

7. **THE TECH STUFF.** No modern winemaking tricks are allowed in making natural wines – no reverse osmosis, no spinning cones, no acid adjustment. Organic and biodynamic wines can still use these modern technologies.

8. **STORAGE.** Natural wines are generally more fragile than organic/biodynamic wines due to their low sulphite content. They need to be stored and transported carefully and are best drunk young.

9. **THE RULES?** Well, that's the thing, with natural wines there aren't any. Unlike organic and biodynamic winemaking, there's no certification. It's about trust between producer, seller and drinker.

10. **THE CONTROVERSY.** Some call natural wines the purest form of wine; others call it faulty winemaking. The truth? When it's good, it's amazing. When it's bad, well, it's just straight up bad.

Wine Wanker Approved List #7: Ten Favourite Organic & Biodynamic Wines

(**Hero bottle** – *Château Maris 'La Touge' Syrah, Minervois-la-Livinière*)

Chinon 'Les Graves', Fabrice Gasnier, Central Loire, France
Uncle Mick and Dad used to sell a lot of Loire red in the wine bar. Some of it tasted like tomatoes to me – quite green and lean. But when it was good, it was great. Chinon's one of the best wine villages in the Central Loire and, like the others in the region, makes its wines from 100 per cent Cabernet Franc. It has an energy and a freshness to it that I can't get enough of, mixing red and black fruit with a sprinkling of fresh violets, herbs and spices.

Soave Classico 'La Rocca', Pieropan, Italy
This is top of the tree of great dry white Soave wines. It was Italy's first wine harvested from a single vineyard and it's all grown on limestone. The grape is Garganega, as it has to be, the flavour is somewhere between rich white Burgundy, crisp Chablis and a dash of zingy Assyrtiko to add a twang. It's so so good.

Gigondas, Château de Saint Cosme, France
Gigondas was one of my early 'go-to' wines. It is often less expensive than Châteauneuf du Pape but with all the heady heat and power I love from the Southern Rhône. Not cheap but Saint Cosme make truly great wines – powerful, brooding monsters that pack in a whole bucket-load of pleasure.

GOOD SHIT

Sonoma Zinfandel, Seghesio Family Vineyards, California, USA
Fully loaded is how I'd best describe this. My first taste of a really good Zin and it's a blueberry fruit-bomb with soft, rich, velvety tannins. It's one of those don't-bother-going-back-to-your-desk-after-lunch wines.

Mature Vine Pinot Noir, Rippon Vineyard, Central Otago, New Zealand
It was when I first tasted this wine that I realised that the Pinot Noir map really *doesn't* stop at Burgundy. This one is right up there with the juiciest, most generous and best Pinot wines I have tried from NZ and it's a banger every time I'm lucky enough to drink it.

Riesling Pechstein GG, Reichsrat von Buhl, Pfalz, Germany
If your perception of German Rieslings is that they're all a bit sweet and light, get your chops around a glass of this and you'll be thinking very differently. The 'GG' in the name stands for 'Grosses Gewächs', which basically means Grand Cru as it is in France. This Riesling is saline, intense, full of zingy grapefruit-like flavour. Quite simply, stunning . . . and it's bone dry.

Cornas Granit 60, Domaine Vincent Paris, France
Cornas is a tiny appellation in the Northern Rhône that produces one of my favourite styles of wine. This red is grown from sixty-year-old Syrah vines (it has to be Syrah) and it's like a liquidised stick of spicy liquorice. All cracked black pepper and black fruit.

Morgon Côte du Py, Domaine Jean Foillard, Beaujolais, France
The Beaujolais region's 'most serious' wine is Côte du Py from Morgon, a single vineyard that produces reds jam-packed with plum, kirsch and deliciously smoky notes. The first time I tasted this wine I was looking at the ceiling for at least two minutes – I couldn't believe it was from Beaujolais.

Pétalos, Descendientes de J. Palacios, Bierzo, Spain
I thought Spain was all about oaky, smoky, soft and easy drinking reds from . . . mainly . . . Rioja – then I came across this. It's about as far in flavour from a Rioja as you can get and it's brilliant for it. It's brimming with fresh acidity, fine tannin, and bursting with bright black fruit – the sort of wine that all Pinot Noir lovers should try.

Crozes-Hermitage, Domaine de Thalabert Paul Jaboulet, Côtes du Rhône, France
This is one of the best-value Northern Rhône Syrahs you can buy. All black olive, black and blue fruits, as a well-made Crozes should be – gosh, I love these wines. This one is a full-bodied brooding monster that'll make you sit up and pay attention from the gun.

8
Wine Money

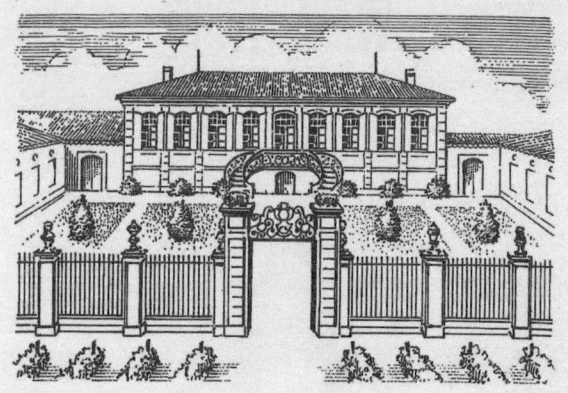

Hero bottle: *Château La Lagune 2005, Grand Cru Classé, Haut-Médoc*

For every delightful new wine discovery, I have five disaster stories. And I've had my fair few of those, too, in trying to make a turn by investing in wine. In fact, at the ripe old age of fifty-three, I'm still trying to get my head around it. There's the 'older is better' myth and yes, maybe some wine does get more valuable with age, and then if and when it does, that investment is exempt from capital gains tax if you're in the UK. That sort of wine is almost too good to be true. Well, as I found out . . . it often is.

Let's start with the 'older is better' myth. There's that saying: 'you can't polish a turd'. You see where I'm going with this? You can age a bottle of plonk for fifty years, and all you'll get is old plonk – that's to say that Blue Nun, that cheap, sickly sweet white wine from Germany, doesn't just magic itself into the most majestic wine of Bordeaux, Château Lafite if you leave it in the back of a cupboard for five years. Of course, some wines *do* improve with age, but they need to be properly good to start with and they need to be well cared for too. And by that I mean they need a bit of structure, the backbone to age: plenty of fruit, acidity and, for reds, a good bit of ripe tannin.

Generally-speaking, though, I maintain that most white wines – anything under £20, really – are better with a couple of years' bottle-age on them, and many reds are better with double that and more (up to ten years). The caveat is that you've got to store them in a cool, dark place, away from a radiator, and preferably on their side if they're sealed with a cork, to prevent it from drying out.

And then there's the investment bit of the puzzle. Yes, some people definitely do make money from investing in wine. These are usually the same people who already have enough money to buy the châteaux that makes it, not just a couple of cases, but it *is* possible.

For the rest of us, it's like joining an expensive wine club where your membership fees are called 'storage costs' and your 'dividend' is in fact the reverse: it's the fee you pay on the way out. To put it another way, imagine winning a free dinner in a fancy restaurant then getting a bill for the chairs, table, cutlery and plates.

So, which wines get more valuable with a bit of bottle age? Not many of the ones I have bought – and I've had a few cracks at it. In short, for wine to appreciate in value it's got to be the absolute best of the very best and, as I've said, it can't have been stored in your kitchen wine rack above the oven. To make money from your investment, potential buyers of aged wine need to know that the wine is in good condition – that it's been stored in a cool, dark place, on its side, and ideally in its original case. And the easiest way of ensuring that is by keeping the investment wine in a bonded warehouse, which is government approved, and you pay no duty or VAT on it until it leaves the warehouse. Importantly, these bond stores are temperature-controlled so offer the perfect conditions for wine storage. This is how many of the wine merchants store their wine and many of them will store their clients' wines there too.

So, it's not quite as easy as it all sounds. What's more, you've got to pay for the storage, of course. It's not like renting out a flat where (ideally) the value of your flat increases while the tenants pay you rent and hopefully don't set the property on fire. No, us canny wine investors *pay* rent (i.e. storage fees) rather than receive it. So, while you're at home turning down the thermostat so you can afford to pay for the bond storage, your investment cases are basking in the wine-equivalent of Barbados – all temperature-controlled, humidity-monitored, and no doubt complete with a complimentary personal meditation guru for good measure. Sometimes I wonder why I don't jump into a wooden box and join my wines in there.

But the really frustrating bit comes when it's time to sell, because it can be a bit like flogging a second-hand car. You get a quote of one figure online, then actually you end up with only 75 per cent of that figure, if you're lucky.

To get the best deal, you often have to sell your wine via brokers, who really are masters of the soft sell. In my experience, they tend to show you graphs of wine prices going up and up and up, and conveniently not show you the ones revealing your storage and insurance costs doing the same.

'This is a once in a lifetime vintage,' they'll say. Or, 'This grower is one to watch out for.' And then by the time you come to sell it, they hope that you'll have conveniently forgotten all that, including what you paid for it, because, surprise surprise, that 'liquid gold' isn't so liquid or so golden as you'd imagined it to be because 'the market's a bit flat right at the moment'. And when I'm wanting to sell, it seems to always be a bit flat.

These days, therefore, I invest in wine the old-fashioned way – I buy it, I drink it, and my return is the memories it creates. That way I might not be on a one-way ticket to make my millions, but at least I don't have to pay a broker to store my memories and they're certainly not getting any commission when I forget them.

I have, though, had one significant win with wine investment. Back in 2007, I got an offer to join my good friend Gavin Quinney (he of that magical anniversary weekend at the beautiful Château Bauduc) at a very special wine tasting in Paris. It was the first time the 2005 Bordeaux Grand Cru Classé red wines were being shown in bottle and Gavin Quinney was on a quest to shake up their scorings.

Bordeaux is the capital of the old wine world. Brits and Americans have loved Bordeaux wine for well over a century and for good reason... the good wines are brilliant. Generous and easy to enjoy. Generally, in my experience, the more you pay, the better the flavour you get, which is more than can be said for Burgundy wine, which is (to me) – only marginally less so than the Italian wines – a minefield.

Gavin is the best taster of Bordeaux wines I know. If you're going to bet the family farm on Bordeaux, Gavin's a good guy to have by your side. A château owner himself, he knows his Pauillac (think cassis, cedar and cigar box) from his Pomerol (think violets, velvet and soft plum fruits), and he, along with every other wine critic in the world, had clocked that 2005 was a quite exceptional vintage, one of the best of the century. He was also blessed with an uncanny ability to predict the American wine critic Robert M. Parker's palate. Mr Parker, at the time, was not just any critic, but the most famous, well-respected and influential judge of Bordeaux wines the world has ever known. Never before or since has the fate of the most important wine region in the world lain in the hands of just one man – it was quite extraordinary. However, Gavin had this theory that at the *en primeur* tasting, the critic had, on this rare occasion, got it wrong on a couple of these wines. This was a rarity, mind you – Mr Parker's mouth was insured for more than most people's cars. But as the wines were not yet the finished product, even the great man was at the mercy of a few uncontrollables.

'*En primeur*? What?' I hear you say. A bit of context and explanation here...

Bordeaux is a funny one. They show their wines to the world first at what we call the *en primeur* tastings. At these first tastings – which are unique, really, to Bordeaux – the wines are shown as barrel samples, i.e. they have not been finished and stabilised for bottling. And it's a complete circus. The circus ringmaster is the Union des Grands Crus (UGC), coordinating tastings of the previous year's vintage while it's still ageing in barrel. These wines are Bordeaux's heavyweight – the AOC classified growths and other top estates – wines that make wine-lovers' hearts flutter and their wallets weep. And for the investment bankers, or investors, in the room: think of it as a bit like futures trading. The châteaux get to set their prices based on early feedback, and the buyers get first dibs at what's meant to be preferential prices. And these wines are the best of the best.

The *en primeur* tasting routine is relentless. Each morning, you rock up to a different château where they've laid out barrel samples from their particular appellation. One year, I remember starting in Margaux. That appellation alone was showing about sixty of their wines. Then we hopped over to Saint-Julien – there were a similar number of wines to taste there, too. Next down to Pessac for more of the same. It's like speed dating with red wine, all of us wandering around like vampires with our claret-stained teeth and gums.

This isn't the sort of event you go to to learn how to taste wine – you've got to know what you're doing. These wines are raw, tannic beasts, and by the end of a big day, if you're anything like me, you're in pain. Some, though, taste brilliant from barrel, while others are so closed and brooding you need to . . . well, you need to eat rather than drink them. You're not alone, though. There are hundreds of bleary-eyed wine buyers, wine critics and journos shuffling between châteaux swirling, spitting and scribbling/dribbling notes about wines that won't even be bottled for months. It's completely mad, in fact – a week of caffeine-fuelled chaos with each of us trying to evaluate wines that won't be ready to drink for years, based on samples that can't really represent the finished blend. But it's also brilliant. Where else do you get to peek behind the curtain at some of the world's greatest wines while they're still getting dressed?

But back to autumn 2007 and Paris, Gavin and I in a tasting room with sixty-one of Bordeaux's finest 2005 vintage. A vintage that was already legendary – one of those years when a Bordeaux winery would have been hard pressed to make a bad wine. But, as I was to taste for myself, some had. Gavin and I weren't there for the mediocre, however – we were there to sniff out the gems that the great Robert Parker might well decide he wanted to reevaluate, once he got to taste them at the official, more comprehensive tasting in London, about five months hence, and a key date for the good and the great of the international wine trade. This Paris tasting that Gavin and I had been invited to was a mere stepping stone for these wines on their journey to greatness.

The tasting room was set up like all good professional wine tastings, everybody dressed up in their smart suits and elegant dresses, standing behind the imposing Bordeaux-laden tables.

'Ready to taste some history?' Gavin laughed, with me trying to look professional while also trying not to pee my pants with excitement. I was about to taste the greatest wines money could buy from one of the greatest vintages of my lifetime with the greatest Bordeaux wine taster I knew . . . and he was my friend, just the two of us together along with all the greatest wine tasters from Paris and beyond.

Everyone here knew Gavin, of course, so it took us some time to make it over to the table of glasses, but I was flying under the radar – I was a nobody, recognisable to no one. I could get on with my tasting without interruption and with no fear of having to offer anybody my notes or opinions.

Gavin passed me the tasting booklet. We each took a clean glass and then for the plan . . .

'Tom, you go round anticlockwise and I'll do clockwise. We'll probably meet around Château Kirwan and we can have a regroup there. Oh, and here's a bit of my prep-work with Robert Parker's scores on the right-hand side.'

Meticulous as always, Gavin had printed out a separate tasting sheet for us both, detailing each of the wines roughly in the order that he wanted us to taste them, each with Robert Parker's earlier score alongside.

'I've left the tasting notes off these because we'll make our own. And I suggest you taste before looking at RP's scores, mark down your own, *then* review RP's score. And then, if you're wildly off, taste again. Then make a few notes. Got it?'

'Easy,' I thought. And I joined the glamorous throng, with a heady mix of excitement, apprehension and panic.

We worked methodically, two wine detectives looking for clues. I started nervously, very unsure of my ability to play this game at this level but by wine number twenty, I got a bit of wind in my sales, or perhaps wine in my bloodstream. 'I've got this,' thought I. I was desperate not to cheat so followed Gavin's instructions to the letter, mostly, and I was matching a few of Parker's scores pretty much bang on. I knew the style of wine he praised – it was everything that every other critic looked for but with added ripeness and generosity, hence the world hung on his every word. About ten wines in, when I hit Château La Lagune, I was stopped in my tracks. Parker had given it a decent score, but this wasn't decent – this was extraordinary. It felt like stumbling into a packed Albert Hall to hear Adele belting out 'Set Fire to the Rain'.

One whiff of this Château La Lagune greeted me with a turbo-charged injection of cassis – proper, straight-off-the-bush blackcurrants. Then the spice – a bit of my grandpa Alan's cigar smoke and a dollop of vanilla on top. One sip and, wowsers, this was different. The wine unfolded on my tongue like a desert flower after rain. The bright black fruit came through and was now joined with violets and truffle. It was quite extraordinary – pure black velvet. None of those grippy tannins that made me crave a cold beer.

I'd found one, I was sure of it.

I sat down on one of the only seats in the room, just me and Château La Lagune 2005, lost in thought for anything but this wine. This wasn't just fermented grape juice; it was liquid poetry. It wasn't showing off, it was just being exactly what it should be – a perfect expression of what happens when Mother Nature blesses great terroir with a really great growing season. And I 'got' it – this great wine was standing out among the good. I could trust myself on this.

Then came another: Château Montrose. A wine that, when young, is only just easier than reading *War and Peace* in the original, but this 2005 was already singing... in perfect English. Parker had been good to Montrose, but I wondered if the score could be even better. It really was that special.

Gavin and I met about halfway round, near the Château Kirwan table. Me beaming my crimson-stained smile with black-striped teeth.

'Getting what I'm getting?' he smiled back.

I excitedly pointed out La Lagune and a couple of others. Gavin highlighted three or four from his side and then we swapped notes.

'I see what you mean.'

'What did you think of Pavie?'

'Go back and taste La Mission Haut-Brion.'

'Have another look at Léoville Poyferré.'

So off I trotted and, sure enough, another look at these wines with Gavin's reassurance and these really were 'sell-your-grandmother's-jewellery' good. He looked at me over his glass and raised an eyebrow. The real fun came in trying to stay professional while doing cartwheels on the inside. The other tasters wore their serious faces and made serious notes. Meanwhile, I was grinning like a schoolboy who'd just worked out how to hack the cigarette machine. We both thought we could make a few quid here.

The big 2005 Bordeaux tasting was in London the

following February. This was the tasting Robert Parker was due to attend, after which he'd probably rescore some of the wines. They would then either go up or down in value accordingly. And if my and Gavin's tasting notes were anything to go by the general trend was going to be up, and their prices would go up too.

Back home in London, I decided to take a punt. I trusted Gavin's palate and I'd become much surer of mine. So sure, in fact, that I unlocked my entire savings and went all in. This was either going to be the smartest wine move I'd ever made or the ruin of me. I bought as many bottles of the great stuff as I could afford – ten dozen Château La Lagune; five dozen-each of Château Montrose and Château Léoville Poyferré; twelve bottles of La Mission Haut-Brion; and I even managed to get my hands on a dozen Château Angélus, too, a wine which is about as rare as rocking-horse shit and *a lot* more expensive (look it up: it's too vulgar to type the price here). These were all top-flight wines that Gavin and I thought were the cream of the cream. Then came the waiting game.

The day Parker's revised scores came out was like waiting for my exam results only different. This time, I felt I had half a chance of passing. La Lagune – up. Montrose – up. Léoville Poyferré – up. La Mission Haut-Brion – up . . . to 100 points! And so on and so on. He had generously revised the scores of all the wines I'd bet big on. It was like a win at the Grand National and the prices moved faster than a sommelier to his tip.

One week in and I sold the lot and, for once, the gold was liquid.

That profit became the seed money for my first wine

company, The Vintner – not a bad return for a couple of days' fun and tasting in Paris.

Gavin and I still laugh about it over a few odd bottles we probably should have sold, too. Then again, wine's about the craic. And of course, things could have gone very differently. Parker could have stuck to his guns, or the market could have shrugged at the new scores and prices, and I could have ended up delivering pizzas in Mozza, my old Morris Minor. But that's the beauty of wine – it rewards those who take the time to understand it, who trust their palate, and who occasionally have the courage (or perhaps madness) to bet big on their convictions. And yes, it also helps to have friends like Gavin who know their stuff and are willing to share their knowledge over a glass or ten.

The Bordeaux 2005 vintage is indeed legendary, and these wines that Gavin and I identified are even more incredible now. But for me, they're more than just great bottles – they were the foundation stones of everything that came after. Every now and then I taste them – not the La Mission Haut-Brion sadly as I couldn't resist selling all of that – and they take me back to that Paris tasting and to the fun I had when I sold it all (well, most of it) and watched the lovely dollars roll in. And I think about what I did with that money – starting The Vintner, in 2010, and with it ten more years of laughter, tears and sleepless nights in this slightly unhinged wine game.

But I'm jumping ahead of myself. Back to more stories of some early disasters. In the wine business, you can't really compare Burgundy to Bordeaux – in a sense, it's tantamount to comparing an Armani suit with a pair of dungarees. Even the way the two wines are classified is different. In Burgundy, it's all about the land. Each individual vineyard has its own classification which might be Grand Cru, Premier Cru, or just the name of the nearest village. Or it might be no village at all. What's more, many different growers here might each farm the same vineyard to produce a range of their own particular wines with a slightly different style and flavour. In short, it really is a minefield, and sometimes you hit a mine.

I hit a mine with a white-wine Burgundy grower in Corton-Charlemagne, one of the largest Grand Crus in the region. The Corton-Charlemagne vineyard is so vast, in fact, that while the higher vines are largely recognised as being Grand Cru worthy, the likes of us wine-trade folk rate the vines lower down as not much beyond bog-standard village Chardonnay level.

In 2004, I bought 600 bottles of this beautifully rich and heady Grand Cru white Burgundy and I had just the customers in mind to buy it. 'They'd love it,' I thought, and I did too . . . at the time of tasting, that is.

Everything went to plan. We sold the lot to very happy customers, some of whom happened to be the Oxford colleges. I'd shown the wine to my friends at St John's College, Oxford – Ian Sobey, the Aussie wine steward, and Professor Steve Davies, the chemistry wizard who bought more wine than all the Oxford colleges put together. We'd gone through the usual dance of tasting and discussing, while they pulled out the odd dusty bottle to 'see how it was getting on', and my Corton-Charlemagne was showing absolutely brilliantly – with loads of citrus and butter and a gorgeous tension between ripeness and freshness that makes great white Burgundy some of the most wonderful wines in the world. The profs were sold, the college was sold – to the sum of 120 bottles. And, trying to look appropriately scholarly, I was mentally doing the arithmetic. This wine cost £70 a bottle – so it really was extra special, and so was the commission I'd be earning off the order.

Fast forward three years. I'm sitting at my desk, probably flicking my pen round my finger and at the same time trying to balance a pencil on my upper lip, when the phone rings. It's Prof Sobey.

Usually when a customer calls a year after buying wine, it's to tell me how brilliant it is and/or to order more. However, this was not that kind of conversation.

'The most peculiar thing,' he said, in that wonderfully measured Oxford way. 'Do you remember that Corton-Charlemagne you sold me? Is it meant to be sparkling?'

I nearly spat out my coffee. 'Sparkling, Professor?'

'Yes, rather. Bubbles. Quite lively ones, actually. We opened it at high table last night and it made quite a dramatic entrance. It upstaged the Master's speech somewhat.'

Grand Cru white Burgundy is one of the most delicious, complex, out and out great white wines in the world and it's supposed to be many things, but 'sparkling' isn't one of them.

'Fascinating really. We've never seen anything quite like it. The junior fellows were quite impressed. They thought I'd invited them to taste a new wine category,' the prof continued, evidently having a bit of sport.

I was sweating now, mentally calculating how many cases I'd sold to the college and wondering if my career in wine was about to go the same way as the bubbles in that bottle – up and out.

But here's the thing about proper wine people – they're often surprisingly understanding about wine's occasionally anarchic tendencies. The maths professor was actually chuckling. 'Reminded me rather of my student days, watching the May morning revellers from Magdalen Tower. All that effervescent energy...'

We figured out what had happened, of course. A secondary fermentation in bottle – the sort of thing that can happen when a bit of residual sugar meets some very determined yeast in a warm spot. Not something I'd come across before in white Burgundy.

The college didn't want their money back (thank whatever wine deity was watching over me that day). Instead, the professor suggested he keep a few bottles back as what he called 'pedagogical examples of vinous evolution' – which I think was professor-speak for 'this will make a brilliant story at the next faculty dinner.'

I learned a few things that day. Firstly, always check your storage temperatures. Secondly, Oxford dons have a surprisingly good sense of humour about fizzy things that aren't meant to be fizzy. And, finally, sometimes the best wine stories come not from the bottles that behave perfectly, but from the ones that decide to go rogue. The prof's phone call that day reminded me that wine, like life, can be full of unexpected effervescence.

The professor still orders from me, though now he occasionally asks, with what I swear is a twinkle in his eye, whether I'm selling any 'naturally sparkling' Corton-Charlemagne. And every time I visit St John's, someone inevitably brings up the Great Fizzing White Burgundy Incident.

I've learned to lean into it – after all, as my old man used to say back in the Eton Wine Bar days, sometimes you've just got to wing it, even when it wings it right back at you.

TEN REASONS WHY YOUR WINE MIGHT SMELL LIKE YOUR GRANNY'S CARDIGAN

1. CORK TAINT (TCA). Cause: fungus attaches itself to a cork and reacts with the wine. Smells like: wet cardboard, musty cellar, damp dog. The verdict: the wine's definitely faulty. Send it back. The restaurant/shop should recognise the problem instantly and replace it.

2. OXIDATION. Cause: too much oxygen got into the wine after sealing, like leaving a cut apple out and it goes brown. Smells like: sherry, old bruised apples, marmalade or nuts. Looks like: a brownish tinge in whites; a brick colour in reds. The verdict: unless it's meant to be oxidative (like sherry), the wine's faulty.

3. REDUCTION. Cause: the wine didn't get enough oxygen during winemaking. Smells like: rotten eggs, struck matches, rubber or maybe farts. The verdict: funnily enough, lots of people don't class this as a wine fault; it will often clear with decanting or some vigorous glass swirling. If the unpleasant odour doesn't blow off though, send it back.

4. VOLATILE ACIDITY (VA). Cause: bacteria have had a party in your wine. Smells like: nail polish remover or vinegar. The verdict: small amounts of VA can add complexity but too much and the wine is definitely faulty. Send it back.

5. BRETT (BRETTANOMYCES). Cause: a specific yeast strain got involved in the winemaking process and had an out-of-control party. Smells like: barnyard, sweaty saddle,

Band-Aid plasters. The verdict: controversial! Some love it (natty winemakers), some hate it (me). High levels are generally considered faulty.

6. **HEAT DAMAGE.** Cause: wine gets overheated during storage/transport. Looks like: a leaking cork, sticky bottle neck. Tastes like: stewed fruit, jam, flat and lifeless. The verdict: the wine is faulty and you definitely don't want to drink it. Send it back.

7. **SECONDARY FERMENTATION.** Cause: some rogue yeasts have somehow made their way into the finished wine and they're at it again. Looks like: tiny bubbles in still wine. Tastes like: spritzy. The verdict: it's a fault in still wines – send it back but beware that some wines are bottled with a bit of CO_2 – for example, Vinho Verde – and these are fine.

8. **LIGHT STRIKE.** Cause: wine was exposed to too much UV light. Smells like: wet wool, cabbage. The verdict: faulty. It's common in clear glass bottles which is why makers of rosé wine would love to use dark bottles . . . but it just doesn't look as pretty. Send it back.

9. **MOUSY TAINT.** Cause: bacterial infection. Tastes like: dead mouse, caged rodent (nice!). The verdict: definitely faulty, and gets worse as you drink it so *send it back* before it does.

10. **COOKED WINE (MADERISED).** Cause: wine gets too hot somewhere along the way but it's not heat damaged. Smells like: stewed fruit, Christmas cake. Looks like: very brown, and watch for a dried-out cork. The verdict: faulty unless it's Madeira!

Wine Wanker Approved List #8: Ten Favourite Bordeaux Wines

(**Hero bottle** – *Château La Lagune 2005, Grand Cru Classé Haut-Médoc*)

Saint-Émilion Grand Cru Classé, Château La Tour Figeac, Saint-Émilion, Bordeaux
This wine has to feature. It's really proper grown-up Saint-Émilion red. Of the region's seventy-one Grand Cru Classé châteaux, it's up there with the very best. Generous with fruit and elegant with its creamy, soft tannins and slightly spicy texture.

Clos du Marquis, Château Léoville Las Cases, Saint-Julien, Bordeaux
This was the first really fine Bordeaux wine that Uncle Mick poured for me – a 'claret' as he referred to it (back then), made by one of the best and oldest growers in Bordeaux, Château Léoville Las Cases. If you've ever wondered how anybody can smell pencil lead in a glass of red wine, shove your nose deep into this.

Château d'Aiguilhe, Côtes de Castillon, Bordeaux
This is a wonder drop, every time. The Côtes de Castillon wine region lies just to the east of Saint-Émilion, so not quite as glamorous and, happily, not quite as expensive, but . . . when a great winemaking team does their stuff here, they make magic. This is a soft, supple and smooth red wine – a completely brilliant example of what Bordeaux can produce at not silly money.

Cru Bourgeois, Château Cambon La Pelouse, Haut-Médoc, Bordeaux
This is the wine I wish my ancestors' Château Loudenne was. Rich and generous with plump blackcurrant fruit and plenty of spicy, creamy oak to wrap around it all, too. This is my 'go-to' if I'm seeking a good value red Bordeaux that will impress at Sunday lunch.

Saint-Émilion Grand Cru, Château Rol Valentin, Saint-Émilion, Bordeaux
I fell in love with the 1999 vintage of this wine on a trip to Bordeaux with Jack. It's a soft, juicy, really plush style that I've found dangerously drinkable on a number of occasions.

Les Pagodes de Cos, Château Cos d'Estournel, Saint-Estèphe, Bordeaux
The second wine of one of the most famous and well-respected châteaux of Bordeaux. We're in Saint-Estèphe here, right at the top of the Médoc which itself is directly above Bordeaux. The style here is full bodied, powerful blackcurrant-like fruit with notes of tobacco and cedar and this wine, Pagodes, is one of my favourites of the region. It's a real treat, especially when it's had a few years (ten maybe) to mature in bottle.

Château La Mission Haut-Brion, Grand Cru Classé, Graves, Bordeaux
Don't go anywhere near this wine until it's old enough to wear trousers. It's my 'money's no object' red wine if ever I could afford to buy it or drink it. It's right up there in quality with

the first growth châteaux of Bordeaux and nearly as expensive too. Its wines are powerful, opulent, multi-dimensional – completely spellbinding in fact. Beg, borrow or steal a glass of this if ever the opportunity arises.

Château Gloria, Saint-Julien, Bordeaux
This is old-school classic Bordeaux from the Médoc that should really be in with the Grand Cru Classé, yet is happily not too silly money. It gives a lovely mouthful of ripe black fruit and has all the cedar and spice on the aroma to let you know it's a classic left-bank Bordeaux. I buy it whenever I see it.

Pomerol, Clos René, Bordeaux
If you want a good-value belter of a Pomerol, the kind that is soft, seductive, elegant and creamy, then head for Clos René. In the very expensive world of Pomerol this is one of the few good-value wineries that do things traditionally and just as I like Pomerol to be.

Petrus, Pomerol, Bordeaux
I've had the opportunity to taste this wine twice in my life. They were 1995 and 1997 vintages and I will never forget either. Yes, I wasn't paying. The wines were unlike anything I have ever tasted. Completely remarkable.

9
Glitz & Fizz

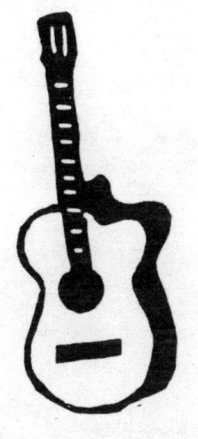

Hero bottle: *Château Palmer, Grand Cru Classé Margaux*

In the seventies and eighties when I was growing up, wine had a very different significance to what it has today. Back then it seemed like it was the epitome of sophistication. Everyone I knew either had it or wanted it. Wine denoted wealth rather than money, and cultural capital – a bit like art – and, alongside James Bond's dry Martini perhaps, it was a subtle sign that you'd *made it*.

Today, the game has changed. There are so many toys to play with, so many celebrities endorsing so many different desirables and, quite frankly, so many great-looking and fabulous-tasting drinks which can put a glass of red wine in the shade. Confusion about what wine should taste like, the monstrous prices of some of them, and the stigma that it's perhaps a bit stuffy, just a drink for dads and grandparents – none of this helps wine's reputation. If I'm not careful I can find it a bit depressing.

Then I remember all the really fun times I've had with wine. Some of the incredible people I've either sold it to, drunk it with or delivered it to.

I've worked for some real characters and with a few celebrities over the years; sometimes we've shared a bottle or two. And for them – from action stars who made their names punching bad guys on screen to cricketers, business tycoons to rock stars – wine has never been just wine. They may not necessarily have grown up with wine or known tons about it, but they've all been curious to explore it . . . sometimes maybe a bit too much. Some seem to have got completely hooked, putting their names to labels and buying wineries: Kylie and her range of wines, Gary Barlow with his organic wines, Snoop Dogg and Sting . . . Others have just really got into wine and buy loads of it. But as a whole, they've all helped democratise wine culture for the better, changing how we choose wine and how we drink it.

I got a surprise one late-summer evening when I got a call from a good friend of mine whose stepdad headed up Sanctuary Records, which until 2007 was the UK's largest independent record label and the largest music management company in the world (now a subsidiary of BMG). Back in 1979, its founders had discovered Iron Maiden in a pub and thus the company named itself after one of their songs: 'Sanctuary' – but that's by the by. The real point is that my friend was ringing to ask if I wanted to be the official wine supplier for the 2008 Iron Maiden 'Somewhere Back in Time' world tour.

My first reaction was one of confusion as to why Iron Maiden wanted any wine at all – surely for them it was all sex and drugs? My next thought was about my cousin Henry, a die-hard Maiden fan who, I knew, would have a fit when I told him about this proposition. He owned every single one of their albums, knew every lyric. And, unlike me, probably already knew that Nicko McBrain, the drummer, used to finish each of his concerts with a glass or two of Château Palmer 1990, Grand Cru Classé Margaux. Very specific but, as my friend now explained, that's his tipple, a top flight wine from Bordeaux, one of the very best, and certainly one of the finest, richest and most expensive Cabernet Sauvignon-based wines from the region. This is a wine found in the cellars of the wealthiest private collectors and glitziest establishments in the world . . . and other places too, I was now learning. Just the thing, it seems, after you've thrashed a drum kit for three hours and are en route to the next gig in Ed Force One – the Iron Maiden jet – flown by their lead singer, Bruce Dickinson.

My imminent brush with Iron Maiden was a moment for both me and the number one fan to savour and so, the minute I'd agreed to the job, I called Henry.

'Henry?' I managed to keep my voice steady, although inside I was cracking up so much that my cheeks hurt. 'You'll never guess who I've just got an order from.'

His familiar grunt came through the other end of the line – his standard reaction to any question that didn't involve tide times. (As I said, Henry had remained immune to the Gilbey family obsession with wine and wine growers and instead had become a professional fisherman, and an outstanding one at that.)

'Nicko McBrain for Maiden's world tour and we're delivering to the Iron Maiden jet,' I burbled.

'You're joking,' said Henry, his voice higher by at least an octave, sounding like that fourteen-year-old lad with his bedroom wall plastered with Eddie posters. 'Actually . . . to Maiden?' he asked, incredulous.

'Yes, yes!' I told him. 'And Bruce is flying the plane. We've got to get four-dozen Château Palmer 1990 to Ed Force One by nine on Thursday morning and they're going to call me at about six thirty to tell me if it's Biggin Hill, Stansted or Farnborough.'

Henry made a noise that was somewhere between a laugh and a sob, then said, 'F**k off! That's soooo cool. Do you need any help? I mean, I know much more about wine than people think and I could do the delivery for you in my van.'

We both dissolved into laughter then, the kind that only shared childhood embarrassments can produce. When we finally caught our breath, Henry cleared his throat. 'But seriously, that is soooo cool. Make sure you get on their tour video.'

I called in multiple favours and tapped a couple of private cellars and I got the wine in on time. Four pristine wooden cases of liquid gold sitting in our temperature-controlled warehouse like sleeping dragons, waiting for the Thursday early-morning call.

We were a tight team and I knew our delivery drivers well. I also knew that one of them, Gavin, was a huge Maiden fan (he had 'Run to the Hills' as his ringtone), so when I rang to offer him the job he nearly crashed his van. I swear he slept in the warehouse the night before, polishing those cases until he could see his face in them.

The call came at 6.32 a.m. Stansted. I can still hear the screech of van tyres as Gavin peeled out of the warehouse. He had strict instructions: 'Don't mention "The Number of the Beast". Don't ask for autographs. Just deliver the wine.' It was like telling our eldest son Freddie not to tell Billy, our youngest, that Father Christmas didn't exist.

Gavin found the jet in good time and found the chaos: the tour manager screamed at him, asking who the f**k he was. Of course, nobody had alerted the tour manager about the impending arrival of the wine order and Gavin had already been told where to go – everywhere and nowhere it seemed – by at least six different people in hi-vis jackets, each more exasperated than the last. So, standing there, surrounded by flight cases, drums, and what looked like enough electrical cabling to power a small city, clutching his delivery note like it was a backstage pass, he tried to explain that he had four cases of Château Palmer 1990 in the back of his van for Nicko. 'Oh, FFS!' came the angry reply.

Then, through the maelstrom of roadies and technicians, emerged a figure he recognised. Bruce Dickinson was striding towards him with purpose.

'Who are you then?' Bruce called out, removing his sunglasses.

'I'm Nicko's wine guy,' bleated Gav, trying not to pee his pants with nerves and excitement.

'Bit early for Château Palmer, isn't it?' suggested Bruce.

Gav had strict instructions not to be a fan-boy and managed a professional nod and a 'Yes, sir. Four cases for Nicko.'

Bruce chuckled, leaning against the van and peering at the cases through the open door. 'You know, I keep telling Nicko he should try Chilean Sauvignon Blanc. Lighter, cheaper, less pretentious. But no, it has to be Palmer '90.' He shook his head like someone who's had this conversation before. 'Though I suppose after three hours of hitting things, he's earned the right to drink whatever the hell he wants.'

Gav was finding his voice: 'It's a beautiful wine, sir. The '90 Palmer...'

'Call me Bruce,' he interrupted. 'Anyone driving four cases of Margaux across London at dawn calls me Bruce.'

'The '90 Palmer,' Gav continued, warming to his subject despite his best efforts to remain professional, 'it's got this incredible power but elegance too. Bit like your music, actually.' He immediately wished he could swallow his words.

But Bruce's face lit up. 'You know your Maiden as well as your Margaux then?' He gestured at the chaos around the plane. 'Go on then, tell me more about this power and elegance thing.'

And there, in the shadow of a Boeing 757 with Eddie in chains painted on the tail, the lead singer of Iron Maiden and Gavin the wine delivery driver chatted bollocks about Bordeaux vintages and heavy metal. Gavin banged on about how the '89 Palmer was like 'Powerslave' – classic, powerful and perfectly balanced – while the 1990 was more 'Seventh Son of a Seventh Son' – complex, layered, and perhaps even more rewarding as time went on.

And then the excitable tour manager came along, totally ignoring Bruce and frantically waving and screaming at Gav to reverse his van if he did actually want to deliver this bleedin' wine. As Gav reversed up to the Boeing, he saw Nicko, one of the world's greatest drummers, waving from the top of the steps, and shouting, 'Oi, boy, is that my Palmer?' Then to Bruce and the others below, 'This, boys, is what keeps the rhythm section properly oiled!'

Gav started up those steps to load the first case onto the Boeing. Inside were red leather sofas, tour schedules pinned to the walls; he said it was like a flying rockstar palace meets a gentleman's club with enough space to host a small in-flight gig.

When Gavin had got the last case safely stowed, Bruce

sidled up to him grinning and said, 'Next time, bring some Chilean Sauvignon Blanc, too. We'll do a blind tasting – Nicko'll never know what hit him.'

When Gav arrived back six hours later he was floating. I've never seen a delivery driver so happy. He'd actually met Bruce Dickinson. Right there on the tarmac in his full pilot's uniform. Chatting about how Bruce can't understand all the fuss about Nicko McBrain's Château Palmer 1990 and how he should be happy with a Chilean Sauvignon Blanc.

I wish I'd been there to see it for myself. I had to calm Gav down with a whisky before he could get the whole story out properly and I'd love to say I got to taste that Palmer but I think the story tasted even better. And, every time I hear a Maiden song now, I think of that very strange and funny moment. One of the world's classic wines being delivered to one of the world's greatest drummers of one of the world's greatest heavy-rock bands. Pure class, I feel, that warms the cockles.

A bit of context here . . . Bordeaux is thought of as the world centre of fine wine, with some of the most famous names in the game. What's less well-known is that the region produces as much wine as the whole of Australia and much of it is very average indeed. The really special stuff is produced just south of the city, in the ACs of Graves and Pessac-Léognan, over the river to the east, in AC Saint-Émilion and AC Pomerol, and, most importantly for this story, on the strip of land to the north of Bordeaux city itself, in the AC Médoc.

The Médoc is unlike any terroir in the world and here its wine producers are ranked a bit like a football league – with Premier Cru Classé being a bit like the Premier League, and the second, third, fourth and fifth sub-divisions underneath. These rankings, known as the 'Grand Crus Classés', were devised by the Bordeaux wine trade according to the prices that the wines were selling for at the time, back in 1855, and the classification system hasn't been tampered with since. (With one exception – in 1972 Château Mouton Rothschild moved up a league, and is now a Premier Grand Cru Classé.) And Château Palmer, Nicko's favourite wine, is classified as a third growth or, in French, a 'troisième Cru Classé'.

And so, here's a story that I hope might tie this all together . . .

One of my favourite and biggest catering customers once asked me to source the wine for a very specific, very VIP dinner they were organising.

The venue alone – Wellington Arch – deserves a plug. It's one of London's most iconic landmarks, an imposing, colossal monument built between 1826 and 1830 to commemorate Britain's victories in the Napoleonic Wars, situated right in the middle of Hyde Park Corner where Park Lane meets Piccadilly. And sitting right at its top, it boasts the most extraordinary dining room I've ever seen. Most Londoners don't even know this room exists and it's very difficult to get permission to host here, so it tends to be used only for very special occasions, diplomatic functions, or extremely high-level corporate events. Surprise surprise, nor had I heard of it before then, let alone set foot inside it, but I knew this job was going to be fun.

My instructions: 'Hi, um, we need the five best wines of France?' said the young, uncertain voice of someone clearly reading from a note. 'For next Thursday?'

I took a deep breath. The five best wines of France. She

might as well have asked me to list the five best paintings in the Louvre, or the five best songs of the 1960s.

'It's a dinner. For some really important people,' she said, then paused, papers rustling in the background. 'Very important actually. Like, really *really* important.'

'I see,' I said, although I didn't see at all. 'You say they specifically asked for the "five best wines of France". Can you tell me a bit more about these really important people? Did they give any preference for the type of wine they're after.'

'Yes! Well, no. They're coming from China and they just said "the *best* wines" – I mean, I *think* they meant the best French wines. But I can't get any more information because they're travelling and unavailable for the rest of the week.'

'So, we assume French?' I said.

'That's right, isn't it?' she said nervously. 'French wine is the best?'

I rubbed my temples . . .

'What's the budget for these wines?' I asked, expecting the usual response of 'Oh, we hadn't thought about that.'

'£12,000,' she replied.

I nearly dropped the phone. That wasn't a budget – that was a signal. Like a secret handshake or a coded message: £12,000 for wine, Chinese businesspeople, 'the best of France' . . . the pieces of the puzzle started clicking together.

'Just out of interest,' I ventured, 'who exactly is the client?'

'Oh, it's a global tech company. From China. They're having dinner at Wellington Arch. Is that helpful?'

And there it was. The final piece of the puzzle. This wasn't just any request for fine wine – this was a *Premier Cru* situation, the five legendary châteaux of Bordeaux's 1855 classification.

The wines that launched a thousand investment portfolios in China.

'The five premiers crus of Bordeaux,' I said, more to myself than to her.

'The five what?'

'I think I know exactly what your clients are expecting,' I said, thinking I didn't have time to explain everything as I just did a few pages earlier. 'Let me put together a proposal. And I'll add some Super Seconds as a comparison? You know, for . . . fun.'

'Super what?'

Today, Super Seconds, the select few deuxième crus châteaux, are widely recognised as producing wines of a similar quality to the premiers crus, or nearly the same quality. But, again, I didn't have time to go into any of that, because I was busy already mentally calculating how many wine cellars I'd need to raid to get this stock in in time. So, I simply said, 'Not to worry. Trust me, I've got this,' adding, 'And there'll be one wine, Château Lafite, that will set the room alight, I promise. Make sure your photographer is well prepped for when we serve that.'

Less than a week later, I was dressed and ready. I'd sourced the five premiers crus of Bordeaux, from those legendary châteaux crowned by the 1855 classification: Châteaux Latour, Lafite, Mouton-Rothschild, Margaux and Haut-Brion. My plan was to serve a Super Second alongside each one. But there was one element I hadn't yet clocked – the language issue. I didn't speak a word of Mandarin, so the whole presentation, I would soon find out, had to be through the company translator, a formal and seemingly efficient lady who seemed to have little interest in wine. This was going to be fun, I thought. Indeed, I was about to experience one of the most surreal occasions of my career, pouring the most expensive and sought-after wines I had ever laid my hands on. Wellington Arch loomed above me in the dusk, its imposing silhouette a fitting backdrop for what was to follow.

Inside and up the stairs, the dining room at the top looked suitably magnificent. Twenty-four place settings immaculately laid, each position bristling with sparkling crystal glassware. Beyond the windows, the lights of Hyde Park Corner twinkled as I scuttled between decanters and bottles, arranging a line-up to impress these really *really* important guests.

They arrived precisely on time. I stood at one end of the room, preparing myself for a stiff evening and, when the guests were seated, my translator introduced me in Mandarin.

When I began my short introductory talk about the wine, the silence was absolute. Twenty-four pairs of eyes focused intently on either me or their phones. After each sentence or two I had to pause to allow the translator to explain the concept: five pairs of wines, each featuring a Premier Cru and a Super Second. A chance to explore, to compare, to challenge preconceptions. They just had to guess which wine was the premier and which was the Super Second. It was, in fact, a simple and great dinner table game if you've got stacks of cash and you're into that sort of thing.

The first pair – Château Latour versus Château Léoville Las Cases – generated polite nods and careful notetaking but absolutely no comment, no conversation, no noise at all. Utter silence bar the clink of a few glasses. The second – Margaux against Rauzan-Ségla – produced a few appreciative murmurs. By the third pair, featuring Mouton-Rothschild and Cos d'Estournel, I'd figured this was the way this tasting was going to be. Not a peep from the guests. Some of the phones had disappeared and interest seemed to be mounting but any actual conversations were yet to begin.

Then came the Lafite.

I hadn't even finished saying the word when the room erupted. Twenty-four previously mute and oh-so reserved executives leapt to their feet as if their chairs had been electrified. 'Château Lafite!' they cried in unison, raising their glasses in a spontaneous toast. Phones reappeared, but this time for selfies. With the wine. With each other. With the wine and each other. With the empty bottle. With the cork.

I stood there, my decanter of Lafite's partner wine – the excellent Château Pichon Longueville Baron – still poised mid-pour, watching as this group of senior business leaders came alive, becoming more excited and garrulous with every sip. My carefully crafted comparative tasting had become a gathering of the Lafite Appreciation Society. I felt so relieved, I nearly burst into song.

Now the translator was laughing. 'They say Lafite is the king,' she explained, as if I couldn't have worked that out for myself. 'The others are just . . . other wines.'

I wanted to protest. To point out that the Château Latour that evening was a significantly better wine with which the Lafite, in this vintage, 1992, couldn't compete. That the Rauzan-Ségla, at less than half the price, was singing like an angel. But there was no point – it would have been easier to push water uphill. Lafite had won this contest before the first cork was pulled.

The final pair – Haut-Brion vs La Mission Haut-Brion – might as well both have been French table wine because the conversation now, so I was told, was all about Lafite prices,

Lafite investments, and Lafite collections. There was no point fighting.

I couldn't help but smile at the absurdity of it all, though. How having just served some of the finest wines ever produced, in one of London's most iconic monuments, in the end the only thing that really mattered was the label everyone already knew. For those of us who aren't transfixed by just the label, there's value in swimming against the tide. Many of the best bottles I've tasted from Bordeaux are either less glitzy vintages or the less glitzy châteaux . . . there's outstanding wine out there that isn't just Château Lafite.

And that's the thing about wine. It still has this power to attract incredible wealth, desire and intrigue. Nicko McBrain knows he likes Château Palmer; the board of a major global tech company in China *love* Château Lafite; someone else might like a bottle of Yellowtail Merlot costing £7.99 from the supermarket, so . . . stick two fingers up to anything that doesn't float your boat, and go buy another bottle of whatever it is that does.

THE IDIOT'S GUIDE TO SERVING WINE – OR HOW NOT TO LOOK LIKE A PLONKER

1. TEMPERATURE MATTERS

- Reds shouldn't be served at room temperature – that is too warm. Ideally, it should be more like cellar temperature, or 16–18°C.

- Whites shouldn't be arctic! Fridge cold, ideally, or 8–12°C.

- Champagne should be properly cold but, again, not frozen, ideally 6–8°C.

- Pro tip: too cold kills flavour; too warm makes the alcohol too prominent.

2. OPENING THE BOTTLE

- Use a simple 'waiter's friend' corkscrew and cut the foil cleanly below the lip.

- Make sure to screw the wine-opener all the way in, and use the lever to gently ease out the cork, rather than yanking it.

- If it's a sparkling wine, hold the bottle at 45 degrees, hold the cork firmly and twist the bottle, not the cork.

3. TO DECANT OR NOT TO DECANT? Do decant if they're young full-bodied reds or to take off the sediment in old reds.

4. GLASSWARE BASICS

- All good wine glasses should taper in at the top.
- Use larger glasses for big reds and smaller ones for whites.
- Flutes or coupes are good for fizz but if you really want to taste it properly use a normal tulip-shaped wine glass. It might not look the fanciest but it works better than both a flute and a coupe.
- Fill to the widest part of the glass (that's about a third full).
- Pro tip: clean glasses matter more than fancy glasses, and make sure they have no residual washing-up liquid in them.

5. THE ORDER OF SERVICE

Like serving a meal: start light and build up.

- Fizz first
- Whites before reds
- Light before heavy
- Young before old
- Dry before sweet

6. THE FIRST POUR

- Pour a bit for yourself first to check it's not corked.
- Then serve others.

- Come back to top up your own.
- Pro tip: use a Drop Stop – it prevents a big mess on the tablecloth.

7. HANDLING THE BOTTLE

- Hold whites/fizz by the base and, once poured, put the bottle back on ice or in the fridge.
- Hold reds around the base.
- When pouring, have the label facing guests – some might be interested in what you're serving.

8. HOW MANY BOTTLES?

A good rule of thumb (bearing in mind there are six glasses to a bottle):

- Over dinner, half a bottle per person, or more if it's a Friday night.
- Over lunch, a quarter-bottle per person (unless it's a Friday, Saturday or Sunday lunch with friends, then all bets are off).

9. STORAGE ONCE OPENED

- Fizz: use a Champagne stopper and it'll keep for up to five days.
- Whites: seal the bottle, pop in the fridge and it'll keep for three to five days.
- Reds: ditto, seal and store in the fridge where they'll keep for three to five days.

- Pro tip: try either a winesave or a Corovin tool, which use argon gas.

10. EMERGENCY TIPS

- No decanter? Use a jug and then pour the wine back into the bottle.
- Wine too warm? Ice bucket with water AND ice for ten mins.
- Wine too cold? Cup the glass in your hands to warm it a little and it'll open up like a flower in spring. (Pay no attention to whatever weird looks you're thrown.)
- Broken cork? Pour through coffee filter-paper.
- No corkscrew? Please don't try the shoe trick – it's better to just gently push the cork into the bottle.

And remember if the bottle's empty, the wine was good.

Wine Wanker Approved List #9:
Ten Classic Wines Befitting a Celebrity

(**Hero bottle** – *Château Palmer, Grand Cru Classé Margaux*)

Braunberger Juffer Kabinett Riesling, Weingut Max Ferd, Richter, Mosel, Germany
In the Eton Wine Bar, we used to serve Piesporter, which is the cheap version of this wine, or let's say 'less expensive'. I loved it and you can still get it in the supermarkets for around £5 a bottle. This is the super-classy version, though. A medium white wine (actually it's really quite sweet), with incredibly fresh acidity too, it's light and full of energy. In fact, it dances along your tongue and is pretty much impossible not to swallow. Think lime-like fruit. It's completely *delicious*.

Wild Sauvignon, Greywacke, Marlborough, New Zealand
Back in my student days, the stand-out New Zealand Sauvignon was made by Cloudy Bay, where the founding winemaker was Kevin Judd. Today, Greywacke is Kevin and his family's project to establish just how good Kiwi Sauvignon can be. This is a *magnificent* wine which, I discovered recently, ages and improves well beyond five years.

Cuvée de la Reine des Bois Châteauneuf-du-Pape, Domaine de la Mordorée, Rhône Valley, France
While Cornas encapsulates the Northern Rhône for me, this Châteauneuf would be my desert-island wine from the south of the region. When I first tasted it in the late nineties, I was stunned, and since then I've enjoyed quite a bit of their less

expensive Lirac. Domaine de la Mordorée make wonderful wines – well worth a try if ever you see them.

Albariño 'Colección', Pazo Señorans, Pontevedra, Spain
Pazo Señorans are at the very forefront of Albariño wines in Rías Baixas, Galicia, northern Spain, where I believe the very best Albariño comes from. This is their 'special wine', a notch above the norm: aged on lees (leaving the wine in contact with the dead yeast cells) to produce something truly outstanding. My favourite expression of Albariño, and a wine I wish I'd found earlier in my life.

Chateau Musar, Bekaa Valley, Lebanon
Here's a wine that everybody should try once in their life. It's a belter of a red made by the Hochar family in Lebanon, who've gleaned much of their winemaking know-how from Bordeaux. I first drank this wine in 1994 and I remember it like it was yesterday. It rivalled the best Bordeaux wine I had yet tasted . . . only bigger, and better.

Pommard Premier Cru 'Clos des Epeneaux', Domaine du Comte Armand, Côte de Beaune, Burgundy, France
I love Pommard as an appellation for red Burgundy. Sitting just to the south of the city of Beaune it conjures up muscular, fleshy Pinots that fill the mouth. This estate is my favourite grower. I just *loooove* this wine.

Condrieu 'La Combe de Malleval', Domaine Stéphane Ogier, Auvergne-Rhône-Alpes, France
I know it's an expensive way to drink peach juice but when I first tasted this wine it really was like the chilled juice of a tin

of peaches. The texture was similar – well maybe not quite so viscous, and the flavours were 80 per cent peach, 15 per cent nectarine and 5 per cent apricot. It's a wine that's stuck in my mind and I look for and choose whenever I can.

Tignanello, Marchesi Antinori, Tuscany, Italy
This Super Tuscan wine is an absolute treat, though sadly a great deal more expensive than it was ten or so years ago. It's broad-shouldered, surprisingly complex and generous – a true beauty.

Gran Reserva 904 'Selección Especial', La Rioja Alta, Rioja, Spain
If you're looking for a red wine that'll give you the ultimate warm friendly hug on a winter's night, this is it – my favourite red from Rioja – expensive but magnificent. It has all the cinnamon, clove and warm winter spices I love from this style of wine, combined with rich, creamy black fruit.

Biondi-Santi Riserva, Brunello di Montalcino, Tuscany, Italy
This is another 'break the bank' red but it's my last recommendation so I'm going with it. If you want to experience just how good Sangiovese from Tuscany can be, go get your mitts on a bottle of this. It is nothing short of *outstanding* and will give any fine wine, made anywhere in the world, a very good run for its money.

10
Blind Tasting

Hero bottle: *Jam Shed Malbec, Argentina*

Over the years, I've learned a great deal about wine tasting from the likes of my uncle Mick and Dad, John at Thames Valley Vineyards, and from Jack Scott, and Gavin Quinney too, after that. Dear Uncle Mick is no longer with us but I hope the man upstairs is treating him to lashings of Saint-Amour. My magical mum is with him, too, I hope, reminiscing about old Eton Wine Bar days and disasters. The others though, who have featured so greatly in my wine life are still at large.

There are many wine tasters out there *much* better than me at blind tasting but I've learned enough now to have the confidence to enjoy it. It's without doubt the most impressive skill any of us wine nuts have up our sleeves, and I continue to learn so much from it. I am so fascinated by *how* I get it right or, more often, wrong. It's a true dark art, or is it?

Blind tasting seems to impress most people, completely flooring some spectators when we get it – or most of it – right. But when we so-called wine experts get it wrong, very wrong . . . that's a different story. We end up the laughing stock of some onlookers in the room (I'd like to see them try it), and the pitied wounded animal to everyone else. To be honest, it's a game I'm always nervous about playing, but if people egg me on enough, my guard slips. And when someone reaches for a new bottle and goads me into 'having a go', well, I will.

Way back when, when I first engaged with this sport, I was always wearing a smart business suit in front of a clique of extremely tipsy corporate revellers, usually baying for blood. After I'd entertained them and their friends for a couple of hours with my own version of a blind-tasting game, some joker would thrust a glass of wine into my hand and challenge me to magic up its vintage, grape variety, its country of origin and precise vineyard, along with the chest size of the winemaker for good measure. Sometimes, well, quite often in fact, it would go a bit awry. Never more so than on the night of Brazilian-Arinarnoa-gate.

I mean, *really*? A *Brazilian* Arinarnoa? When I was first learning my trade, I knew of only a single Brazilian wine which was exported to the UK, and it was made by John Worontschak, at that time my Aussie winemaker boss at Thames Valley Vineyards. He would be the first to admit that it left a little to be desired, but Tesco sold it for £4.99 a bottle by the tank load.

It was 2010 and I was hosting a business wine event, entertaining this group of fifty alcohol-fuelled enthusiasts, when, predictably, someone handed me a glass of this deep dark-red wine. It was time for my blind-tasting trick. Full of youthful confidence, I dived straight in. First, I mulled on that deep-red colour; so deep it was almost black. Red wines get their colour from the skins of the grape: the darker and thicker the skins are, the more colour they leach as they ferment. For this reason, I figured this wine was made from a grape variety with very thick and very dark skin. I therefore ruled out Pinot Noir, Grenache, Nebbiolo and a few others. And I was considering a Syrah, a Cabernet, or perhaps a Malbec or Tannat. It could have been so many more, but that's what I was thinking.

Next I smelled. This almost black wine smelled of . . . a cross between my rubbish bin and a mouldy fruit bowl. I was getting sewage water, still, with a redcurrant floating on the top. This aroma told me nothing at all except that I really didn't want to put it in my mouth. To play this game, I had to, though. So, in it went, and round and round I swished as I had to in order to taste it properly, and . . . it had a fair whack of tannin, that grippy, dry sensation that sucked the saliva from my mouth and sent my tongue flipping around like a dog with a wasp in its mouth. Meanwhile, the fruit was almost too frightened to properly show its face.

I need to pause here as I write, because just thinking about this incident still makes me sweat.

Anyway, now the raucous fifty-strong rabble had fallen quiet in anticipation, awaiting my learned analysis of the mystery wine. But I waited. Took my time. I smelled and tasted again.

'It's a young wine – a 2008,' I announced. 'It's a deep colour so I'm thinking definitely not a Pinot Noir, nor a Nebbiolo, nor a Grenache. It *could* be a Cabernet. But it hasn't got the blackcurrant fruit for a Cabernet and the tannins are too strong. So, I'm going for a Tannat grape. I'm going for France as it's quite grippy and tannic, and I'm saying Madiran – a village in Gascony, a region in the south-west making chunky, robust wines. Is it Château Montus?'

Complete silence in the room. My spectators were all

willing me to have impressed them and I was quietly confident that I'd nailed it. Then off came the cover to reveal the bottle. And there it was: an Arinarnoa, from Brazil. A wine more different from Château Montus would be hard to imagine. I couldn't have been further away from France if I'd tried. Yes it was spicy, gutsy and full bodied but in hindsight it tasted nothing like Château Montus – a fine wine that needs ten years in the bottle if you're not going to have purple teeth for a week after drinking it. Why had I tried to show off and gone for such an obscure wine when I could have saved just a little face by naming something more mainstream? And why on earth had I gone for a Tannat? And I still had to send an invoice to this business for their wine entertainment that evening.

Maybe it was the trauma of my Brazilian-Arinarnoa-gate humiliation; maybe I just wanted to keep learning, but in 2013, I took the plunge and I enrolled at the Institute of Masters of Wine (IMW) in London's Nine Elms, to study for the pinnacle of wine qualifications throughout the world. As I write, there are just 416 Masters of Wine spread across the globe. The number is so low for a few reasons, but as I can attest, it's among the most gruelling courses any crazy wine person can take. Of course, I haven't done many others to compare, but let's just say that it's widely recognised as being a beast.

It's billed as 'a self-study programme that you can complete in three years' – but who 'you' refers to I don't know as most people take between five and seven years to gain the qualification, with multiple retakes and 'time off' for trauma along the way. In short, the IMW has devised a rigorous set of exams which are very difficult to pass, three of which are very challenging, terrifying in truth, blind-tasting tests...

Instructors took pains to drill into us students that it's less about being right and much more about the process although I've never met anybody who's passed the programme having misidentified the wines in the various blind-tasting examinations. To add to the pressure, these are timed tests during which you simultaneously have to scribble all your reasoning alongside your answers. To follow the process and get the right result while watching as the seconds tick by on the clock requires the confidence of a peacock, the analytical skills of Sherlock Holmes, and the creative storytelling ability of Roald Dahl. Not an easy feat.

In the first year, the tasting test involves twelve wines, which could be white, red, rosé, sparkling or orange wine, or a sherry, port, Madeira... the list goes on... In other words, any wine under the sun, and to complete the first stage of the Master of Wine programme, we had to identify them all, listing the grape, country, region, year and alcohol level. To pass this tasting exam is beyond difficult. We were expected to be able to take each wine apart, break it down and put it back together again with a coherent reasoning.

So, there I was, with one year's hard study behind me. I'd submitted my six pieces of written work, and completed my two theory essays under exam conditions. Now I was bracing myself for my first big blind-tasting test. I think I'd have been less nervous if I was standing on the shore at Dover prepping to swim the channel and I seemed to have forgotten everything I knew and believed about how to prepare for a blind wine tasting. I faced my first conundrum before I left the house. The exam was first thing, shortly after teeth-brushing time. Should I use toothpaste as normal? It was possibly the worst thing I could put in my mouth before a wine tasting. So, no toothpaste on the brush that day and it tasted horrible. 'Yuck. How disgusting,' I thought to myself, but this was my big day. I had to nail this. Then the next dilemma. Should I have a coffee? What if I burn my tongue? This was beginning to get silly. I had lost all sense of proportion and all self-confidence.

Outside a beautiful summer's morning awaited me. My destination for the exam was the Mermaid Centre in Blackfriars. At the best of times, not one of London's most beautiful buildings and more like a torture chamber to me that day.

When I got there, I studied the room plan and located my desk number – thirty – just one of the rows and rows of tables each waiting for a dozen tasting glasses to be laid out before a swarm of ant-like wine pourers pounced to fill them up. (I'd brought my own set of trusty, well-worn tasting glasses. I figured tasting with brand-new, unfamiliar glasses would be like running the marathon in a new pair of running shoes.) Soon enough, I was staring at my twelve wines, and they all seemed to be winking at me, each one potentially a career-altering humiliation in the making.

I'd prepped for this moment for months. I'd tasted wines for breakfast, lunch and supper. For the last year, on Saturdays I'd travelled to far-flung corners of Sussex, Berkshire and London to join my fellow Master of Wine hopefuls for blind-tasting practice. I'd become a weirdo who would carry two boxes of specialist wine-tasting glasses, a spittoon and tasting book to a family Sunday lunch. I couldn't even enjoy a cup of builder's tea without analysing every element of its flavour. At school my youngest son Billy, then just ten years old, had started drawing pictures of me with a glass in hand, with the title 'Daddy at Work Again'.

I *had* to make it all worthwhile. But my impostor syndrome was working overtime. Memories of everything I hated about school came rushing back to me. My hands were shaking – perfect for swirling the wine perhaps but I didn't think so at the time. The white exam paper was pristine, crying out for some of my gibberish. I looked around the room at my fellow candidates. Of course, they were probably as nervous as I was, feeling exactly the same inadequacies, but I was sure they were better prepared. Their wild-eyed looks told of a year spent memorising soil types in Burgundy and the pH levels of Picpoul de Pinet, topics which had dominated our Saturday wine-tasting socials.

The bright morning sunlight beamed through the windows, highlighting twelve brilliantly different shades of red, yellow, green, brown, black and purple in front of me. The invigilators, all Masters of Wine themselves, prowled between the tables, their expressions neutral, just waiting perhaps for one of us, probably me, to identify the pale, elegant and delicate red Pinot Noir as a big ballsy Aussie Shiraz.

'You may turn your paper over,' came the ominous words. 'The examination starts now.'

The hall was silent except for the gentle swooshing as we examinees swirled the wines.

'Remember,' I told myself, 'if it walks like a duck and quacks like a duck, it's probably a duck.'

Our Master of Wine studies had started with a five-day residential course in an Austrian town called Rust. Those were among the most gruelling five days of my life, and while

I'd forgotten most of what I'd learned there, I remembered one instructor delivering that line about ducks. 'Don't overthink it,' was the message, because that's when things start to go wrong. And that's still my mantra today.

The first wine winked cheekily at me once more from its glass. It was clear, bright, and a pale lemon in colour. Standard stuff. *But is it? Or is it lemon-green and is lemon-green even a thing? Shit! Have I forgotten how to see colours?* Trying to stay calm, I breathed deeply then I took a sniff . . . *Citrus, stone fruit, mineral notes. Remember that duck, remember that duck . . . Could this be an unoaked Chardonnay, neutral on the nose . . . So, maybe a Pinot Grigio? But it's not aromatic enough to be a Sauvignon Blanc. A Viognier?* . . . And then I wrote my long list of what it was not and carried on sniffing down the line.

I looked around the room nervously and constantly to see everybody else methodically tackling the examination wine by wine – swirling, looking, swirling, smelling, swirling, then tasting before moving on to the next. I, on the other hand, took a different approach. I was doing the look and the smell of the whole lot before tasting anything – getting my eye and nose in first, before going in for the kill and having an actual taste of each wine. At that moment, I remember it being like my entire wine career was flashing before my eyes, twelve times over, as I tried to recall everything I'd tasted, in every region I'd travelled to, hoping that my recall and my palate didn't let me down.

In went the first wine . . . swirl, suck, then around my mouth I sent it, like a washing machine. Out it then came, clean as a whistle, into my trusty spittoon, which I'd brought myself of course, along with my glasses. I looked to the ceiling in despair. This wine was fresh, crisp with gooseberry- and apple-like fruit and now had a smack of freshly cut grass on the nose. It tasted just like a good Sauvignon Blanc from the Loire – in fact, *exactly* like that grape variety I thought it couldn't possibly be only five minutes ago. My confidence was evaporating faster than my aunt Mary's Harvey's Bristol Cream on Christmas Day.

'Don't worry,' I told myself. 'Just press on and get confidence where you can get it.'

And so, to wine number two which tasted like it looked – a light, juicy New World Pinot Noir.

I was feeling a bit more confident. Perhaps I'd swallowed a bit just to calm my nerves or maybe I'd grown calmer as time went on, but now I was getting into my swing.

Wine three was a deep ruby-purple in the glass and a classic Northern Rhône sprinkling of black pepper and blackcurrant on the nose. Everything pointed to a high-quality, fairly youthful Syrah.

'I've got this,' I thought to myself as I took a good large sip to make sure I had a proper 'go on it'. And I did have a proper 'go on it'. Not the go on it I'd intended, though, because at least half had shot straight down my windpipe. I got a good lung-full of fine red then unloaded half of it in loud splutters which landed all over my once clean, white exam paper. Now it sported a deep-purple Abstract Expressionist splodge. The entire exam hall was now much more interested in death by Syrah on table thirty, while my nearest invigilator glowered at me. I'd just flunked the first basic of blind tasting – get it down the right pipe! The number three wine clearly had good intensity to it though – it brought out an intense reaction in the taster. Yes, I'd plump for a Syrah for that one.

A couple more sneaky swallows to calm my nerves and it slowly got better. By wine eight I was relaxed and properly going for it. And by the final taste, it was me showing those wines who was boss. Right or wrong, I was sticking to my ducks.

And job done. I had finished the tasting. My teeth were so deeply stained they'd have made my dentist cry and my mouth felt like it had been carpet-bombed, but there was no turning back now.

Outside, I gathered with my fellow Master of Wine wannabes who were already swapping notes about what wine was what. Wine number seven was definitely a Condrieu, a rich, creamy, peach-like white from the Northern Rhône Valley, which confusingly is in the south of France. No, it was a Chardonnay. Whoops. I'd pinned it as a Roussanne from the Southern Rhône. This was not a fun game – panic was beginning to set in again, so I figured the only thing of which I was absolutely certain was that I needed a cold beer – no tasting notes or analyses required – on my own. And I've never before or since had a beer quite like that one, a long cold antidote to stained teeth and a sandpapered tongue. The entire time I savoured that pint I marvelled about that blind-tasting exam and what a humbling experience it had been.

A few months later while on holiday with the whole family, I got the news. I'd passed. I was ecstatic. We were all ecstatic, I think. My hard work and Beth and the kids' patience had paid off, but it had been quite a year of it. I'm no academic (I've known this for some time), so at dinner that night I announced that that was it for me. No way could I put them, or me, through another two (let alone seven) years of that kind of stress. I'd proved to myself that I could hold my own in a crowd of wine nuts and that was enough for me. I didn't need to be the best blind taster in the business, nor the most knowledgeable wine person on the planet, neither of which I had any chance of being. I had other fish to fry – our four children and shelves full of wines to buy and to taste at my leisure – and not against the clock.

But I was glad I'd made it that far on the Master of Wine course. The 2010 Brazilian-Arinarnoa-gate upset is fifteen years in my past, and since then, having endured that Master of Wine blind-tasting ordeal, I've fine-tuned the art of not looking like a complete arse when I have absolutely no idea what the unknown wine might be. It taught me how to break things down and look at each element of a wine on its own. It taught me humility and it gave me the chance to prove to myself that if I really put my mind to it, I could knuckle down and mix it with the best.

In over thirty years in the business, like these blind tastings, I've managed to muddle through. I've ridden the highs with the lows and, with time, grown to understand and appreciate them for what they are. In my experience, neither lasts forever, so enjoy the good times when they're just that.

My career in wine spans the early days working for Mum, Dad, Uncle Mick and Aunt Lin in the Eton Wine Bar, to my adventures with the influential characters who formed and moulded the man I've become – among them I count John Worontshak and Vince Gower at Thames Valley Vineyards; the inimitable Jack Scott of Jascots Wine Merchants, along with his mum's green Bentley; vintner and master-taster Gavin Quinney; the experiences I've had with Bertie Eden at Château Maris and Xavier Amirault at Clos des Quarterons in the Loire, to name just a few. Amazing, wonderful, passionate characters, all of them.

And today, as of 2021, it's me and our eldest son Freddie, aged twenty-seven at the time of writing, and now my business partner. Never in a million years did he ever envisage working with me, nor me with him. But just as Mum and Dad must have felt when I started working for them, it feels like it's gone full circle. They taught me so much, but I hope I taught them just a tiny bit in return. Now, as Fred learns from me, he teaches me so much more, constantly questioning, challenging, inspiring and surprising me. He never fails to delight me, coming up with fresh ideas that push boundaries.

And so it was that Fred, without too much thought it seemed, came up with the idea for my latest, even more high-risk antics involving wine. You'll have heard about wild swimming, well, I'm talking about wild blind-tasting. No cosy restaurant or wine-tasting room, Fred challenged me to go *way* out of my comfort zone.

If you have this book in your hand, the chances are that you have heard about or seen a social media clip or two of me indulging in my specialist sport, namely someone thrusting mystery glasses of wine at me – sometimes when I'm out running, sometimes shivering in an ice bath, sometimes swimming in the sea. It's the party trick that keeps giving and, to my mind, the most enjoyable way to get into a fight with a glass of wine about which the only thing I can be really sure is the colour.

Fred's latest marketing idea was a crazy one, 'blind tasting in the wild', but perhaps in reaction to those other times in my life when blind tasting felt like walking the plank, this sounded more fun. And it is.

BLIND TASTING

The first of these escapades became a landmark in my working life – the 2024 London Wineathon . . . also known more formally as the London Marathon. But why do a blind tasting while running a London Marathon? Well, I was running it anyway, to raise money for Sobell House Hospice, where the staff had cared for my wonderful mum in her last few days. To guarantee my place, I'd just scraped the necessary minimum £2,000 sponsorship, but now I really wanted to get more.

It was Freddie who rather cheekily pointed out that, at the ripe old age of fifty-two and not being a runner, nor having done much training, I might not win or possibly finish this marathon, so he suggested we add an element of comedy to raise a bit more money.

'Let's get you blind tasting four wines during the race,' he suggested.

Utterly ludicrous, but there was no doubt in my mind that Fred was on to something with this. So, I said yes. I was up for it.

'Great Fred, but let's go "all in" and raise as much money as we can. I'll do twenty-six wines,' I suggested. And so we came up with the plan: I would taste a different wine each mile along the route.

'I'll get some of my and Mum's mates [he doesn't think I have any] to stand along the road,' Fred said, 'and they can pour you a wine that I send them a few days before the race or they can buy their own. And I'll get T-shirts printed and we can have some flags made so you can spot them along the way. Oh, and how about we brand it all up as "The Wine Wanker" and you run as that?'

I knew that tasting/drinking wine along a marathon

course was completely normal for the Bordelais. They run the Marathon du Médoc every year in September while drinking full-bodied red Bordeaux and eating oysters, baguettes and lashings of pâté . . . Surely I could compete in London and blind-taste twenty-six wines?

Fred got to work. He selected the support team and organised the wines. He created a WhatsApp group, and designed and ordered thirty 'Wine Wanker' T-shirts and thirty matching 'Wine Wanker' flags on long poles for the support team to hoik over the crowds. On the Tuesday before the run, the booty arrived. T-shirts and flags distributed. Tick! Now, all we needed was to get the runner, me, to the start line in Greenwich Park, on time, and guess the grape variety, country and year each wine was made, with no clues or tips beforehand from Fred.

That day, Sunday 23rd April 2024, we learned that the world doesn't just love a nutter: it loves nutters, plural. Beside me ran the Blackpool Tower, a camel and a man with a fridge on his back, and the crowd seemed to love us all. Four nutters doing our thing, though I was surely the sanest among us. I learned also that wine tasting (and swallowing) is no hindrance to getting round a marathon. A few days earlier, someone had sent me an article about how, apparently, the winner of the 1924 Summer Olympics marathon had been fuelled on red wine and so I started with a degree of reassurance. I was more concerned about missing my plotted twenty-five wine stops, or misidentifying the wines, which I'm sure helped me get round the route, and get round I did.

In all my exhaustion, for the actual blind-tasting part of this endurance course, I had to keep calm. Each time I stopped to taste, hundreds of runners passed me by, offering me lots of cheers, much laughter and not a small amount of surprise. Quite a few stopped to ask what I was up to. For all the fun, though, my friends had sponsored me to get the wines right – the more I named correctly, importantly, the more money I would raise for Sobell House Hospice. I had to be methodical, so I'd stop, settle myself, then dive straight in using the same method I've been using since my wannabe Master of Wine days – colour, any outstanding smell (other than my sweat), acidity, mouthfeel, any particular fruits, etc., etc. Then calmly write down my answer and keep running to the next wine stop.

Finally, four hours and forty-one gruelling minutes later, I staggered across the finish line, where Fred was set to meet me with the twenty-sixth wine. But there was no Fred. And no final glass of wine . . . which he'd promised would be special – he had sugared off home thinking it was all getting a bit busy.

So, finishing medal round my neck, and walking a bit more wobbly than all of my fellow runners, I headed with the masses to the tube, feeling surprisingly spritely and looking forward to that twenty-sixth glass that Fred now assured me would be waiting at home . . . in west London, so very close. And it was, a glass of perfectly chilled Nyetimber Blanc de Blancs. I shared the bottle with all the team who were there waiting to toast my heroic return. All my wine pourers in their Wine Wanker T-shirts and waving their Wine Wanker flags. And now I got the big reveal – seven wines spot on, as in the country, grape variety and year all correct. Four completely wrong, as in I got everything wrong. And fourteen partially correct. The party had started.

Monday morning was not so great. I couldn't walk and I

think the hangover was finally starting to kick in. Fred suggested he take a couple of hours quietly on his own to collate some of the video clips to raise a bit more sponsorship money. At midday, he showed me the result which he would post on our social media accounts.

'You can't put that out there Fred, it's too silly,' I said.

'Well, the trouble is, Dad, I just have . . .'

And so began the craziest and busiest week of my life. Think Eddie the Eagle, the British ski jumper from High Wycombe who rose to fame on borrowed skis during the 1988 Calgary Winter Olympic Games, coming last and hitting the headlines as a sporting hero. My London Wineathon was featured on television, I did interviews for every podcast and radio station I'd imagined, from London to Sydney, Auckland to New York and more. In short, I was experiencing what it was to go viral. And the greatest thing about it all . . . when I crossed the finishing line, our fundraising stood at £2,745. By the end of that week, we had banked over £38,000 for the hospice, in all currencies, along with messages of support written in sixteen different languages.

HOW TO BLIND TASTE WINE...
UNDER PRESSURE

Quick tilt of the glass and visual check – look at the colour, the intensity and the clarity – rule out what it's obviously not.

1. **SWIRL THEN FIRST SNIFF** – trust your instant reaction: key markers jump out straight away.

2. **SECOND SWIRL AND SECOND SNIFF** – anything new? Anything further to rule out?

3. **STOP**, and take a moment before tasting. Then it's small sip time, and quick sweep: note the acidity, tannin, alcohol, and body of the wine – like you're checking out its vital signs.

4. **RAPID FLAVOUR CHECK/MID-PALATE ASSESSMENT** – register fruit tastes and any secondary flavours like vanilla, caramel, butter, earth, but don't overthink it.

5. **FINISH FLASH NOTE.** What's the quality like? The intensity, the length and the final flavours while moving towards your conclusion.

6. **ELIMINATION TIME.** Where is the wine obviously not from? Start ruling out countries and regions.

7. **THE GRAPE VARIETIES.** What's it not?

8. **IN FOR THE KILL.** You will probably still have multiple possibilities in your mind, but you've got to go for it. Trust your gut and name that wine.

Wine Wanker Approved List #10: Ten Favourite Wines I've Blind Tasted... Correctly

(**Hero bottle** – *Jam Shed Malbec, Argentina*)

Schist Chenin Blanc, Mullineux, Swartland, Western Cape, South Africa
Taste anything made by Chris and Andrea Mullineux and you've got an idea of just how good South African wines are – just incredible, in fact. Intense, complex and completely seductive... until I tried this wine, I really didn't know Chenin Blanc could achieve these heights.

Mercurey Premier Cru 'Clos Des Ruelles', Château de Chamirey, Burgundy, France
If you want top-flight Pinot Noir from Burgundy but can't justify the crazy prices, go for this. It's an utterly charming red Burgundy from a great, great grower in the Côte Chalonnaise, just a bit further south than the Côte d'Or. It's their single vineyard wine and their most charming and seductive... every year.

Barbaresco DOCG, Produttori del Barbaresco, Piedmonte, Italy
If Barolo is the Bordeaux of Piedmonte, Barbaresco is its Burgundy. Both DOCGs use Nebbiolo for their wines but Barbaresco is a more elegant and delicate style. It's gentle, with softer tannins and a touch more fruit. This is made by the brilliant co-op, Produttori del Barbaresco, and I'd recommend all of their wines – they're scrumptious.

Coteaux du Layon Saint-Aubin, Domaine de la Bergerie, Loire, France
Let's go to the Loire for one more glass . . . a sweet wine for dessert or maybe, as the French enjoy it, with *pâté de foie gras*. It's clean and fresh but with moreish, honeyed, citrus fruits. It wins the dancing competition when matched with an apple tarte tatin, so off you pop and rustle one of those up too.

Vina Seña, Seña Wines, Aconcagua Valley, Chile
The team at Seña prove that Chilean winemakers can create world-class wines. It's a Bordeaux blend with Cabernet Sauvignon at its heart – powerful, chocolatey and brambly. Wild and untamed, perhaps because it's got a bit of Carmenère in the blend but, although quite pricy, this wine is terrific value considering its deliciousness.

Brolettino Lugana, Ca' dei Frati, Lugana di Sirmione, Italy
It's not all about Pinot Grigio for whites from Italy. Not at all, in fact. At Ca' dei Frati, on the shores of Lake Garda in northern Italy, the Dal Cero family make wines that'll set your pants on fire. Most of them are whites and this Brolettino is my favourite, but have a 'go' on their Ronchedone red too – it's a fabulously expressive wine – all dark cherries and chocolate.

Le Serre Nuove dell'Ornellaia, Ornellaia, Bolgheri, Tuscany, Italy
I am a big fan of second wines and this one's one of my favourites. It's made by Ornellaia in Bolgheri, home to some of the most magnificent and majestic wines of Tuscany. Blended

from Cabernet Sauvignon and Merlot, it offers everything as wonderful as the very best wines of Bordeaux . . . with an added dollop of generosity and richness.

Grüner Veltliner Ried Renner, Schloss Gobelsburg, Kamtal, Austria
These guys are the kings of Austrian Grüner Veltliner and this wine was a revelation to me. Almost like a rich white Burgundy, but as if somebody had sprinkled white pepper on the top and dropped a tangerine into it. A wonderfully fruity, spicy and intriguing dry white.

Riesling Cuvée Frédéric Emile, Maison Trimbach, Alsace, France
I've already raved about this wine, but buy any wine from the Trimbach estate and you'll be happy. They're pure, generous and incredibly tasty.

Santorini Assyrtiko, Santo Wines, Greece
I first described this as 'a Chablis meets a Clare Valley Riesling' and every time I drink a glass I enjoy it more and more. It's grown on the volcanic soils of the Aegean island of Santorini. It's very fresh in acidity with a life and energy to it that's completely unique. It's all green apple and tangy citrus fruit making it *the* most perfect wine to drink with seafood.

Afterword

If you've got to here and learned a bit along the way, thank you. A really big thank you and I hope that you might have had at least one chuckle or yearning too . . . for a wine that is.

For years I have been told that wine is too boring for many of us to care. It's not colourful or pretty enough to be on telly, it's too expensive and elitest to write about in any widely read publication, it's a drink for old people.

It's clearly time to stick two fingers up to that. The wine bars and new casual dining slots of London and cities across the world are heaving. It's a joy to see them full of people, many with a glass of wine in hand – red, orange, sparkling, white, natural, biodynamic . . . all sorts . . . they're all wines, most made with passion and most speaking of a place, a moment and a people. The wine growers and the drinkers, they're energetic, interesting and interested in what they're creating and enjoying. All ages, all backgrounds getting into wine and its vibe.

Wine is winning. It's winning in these bars and it's winning in our supermarkets and independent wine shops, the 'indies'. Quality is going up, stuffiness is going down, the old guard are giving way and we're invited to taste all sorts of stuff – to experiment.

I'm lucky, I know – I've been dragged up surrounded by wine and food all my life and I've tasted some incredible

AFTERWORD

wines. Never in a million years, though, did I think I'd be writing a book about it all, nor did I imagine that I'd be meeting such interesting and interested people who all seem to want to share their wine experiences. There are lots of us out there, so keep the faith.

My one sadness . . . that my dear mum never saw this all blow up. In fact, she never even saw the hair – she might not recognise me now. But you lot have seen the hair and you lot have made this blow up and you lot, I hope, will continue with me on my quest to stick a rocket up the arse of wine. Let's blow it open, spray it around and learn loads about how truly wonderful it is.

Glossary

BIODYNAMIC WINE: This is essentially a totally holistic farming method treating a farm or a vineyard as its own ecosystem. It encompasses all the principles of organics and more, following the lunar cycles, respecting planetary positions, using energy flows and other fascinating practices to create a robust and healthy ecosystem.

CHAMPAGNE: Must come from the region of Champagne and be bottle fermented. Different from Prosecco which has a second fermentation in tank. It's the benchmark of quality sparkling wine production and the style that's emulated throughout France (in their Crémants) and around the world. Look for Méthode Traditionelle or Méthode Champenoise which tells you that it's made in the Champagne style. Serve well chilled but not frozen, ideally 6–8°C.

CORKED: The unmistakable smell of wet cardboard, musty cellar or damp dog – it's caused by a bacteria reacting with the cork. The full name is 2,4,6-trichloroanisole (TCA) and it can be either mild or honking. The more you taste the better you'll get at whiffing it out.

CRU: Can mean all sorts of things. It literally translates as 'Growth' and, in general terms it indicates good/better

GLOSSARY

quality. It's principally a French term and refers to a vineyard, a village or a château that's been classified at some stage. For example, Château Lafite is a Premier Cru Classé in Bordeaux and Fleurie is a Cru village of Beaujolais.

DOUBLE DECANTING: Exactly as it sounds and you'd do it to either draw sediment off a wine or give the wine a quick burst of oxygen to open it up. Young red wine can taste very tight and tannic at first but given a blast of oxygen it softens up a treat. You can of course decant it once, leaving it in the decanter and serve from there, but if you want your guests to know what you're serving them, decant it back into the clean bottle and sock it to them.

LEGS: Also called 'tears'. These are the lines that form on the inside of the glass after you've swirled it around. The thicker they are and the slower they run down the glass, the higher the alcohol or sugar in the wine.

MAGNUM: Twice the size of a regular bottle, often more than twice the price and always more than twice the fun.

MALOLACTIC FERMENTATION: All wine gets one fermentation, turning sugar into alcohol, but red and some whites get a malolactic fermentation as well. This is when bacteria in the wine turn malic acid (think green apple) into lactic acid (as found in milk). It softens flavours, bringing the perception of acidity down. This is a common practice in most if not all red wines and many cool climate Chardonnays (e.g. lipsmackingly juicy white Burgundy).

GLOSSARY

MUST: A grape juice with all the bits that come with it before it's been filtered or fined. It's the nourishment that the yeasts feast on to turn it into wine.

OENOLOGY: A term that wraps up everything to do with studying wine and winemaking.

ORANGE WINE: A white wine made like a red wine. Red wine gets its colour from the black skins of the grapes. Orange wine gets its colour from the yellow skins of the white grapes. Also known as skin contact wine, it has a full flavour and slightly grippy tannin element to it that bridges the gap between white wine and red.

NATURAL WINE: It's pretty impossible to define natural wine as it has no parameters. It's organic certainly but not necessarily biodynamic. Think minimal intervention . . . so minimal use of sulphur dioxide, filters, fining, etc., etc.

ROSÉ WINE: Rosé is made like a white wine, but from black/red grapes. For red wine the skins are in contact with the juice for the entire fermentation. For rosé it's often just a few hours.

SABRAGE: This is the fanciest, most theatrical way of opening a bottle of Champagne. It's severing the neck of the bottle by gliding a sword or a knife of some sort along the bottle to clip the lip of the neck. The pressure in the bottle takes the top clean off. **Don't try this at home.**

GLOSSARY

SULPHITES: Like bouncers at a party, sulphites are added to wine to keep the bad stuff (like spoilage and bacteria) out of the bottle. You'll find higher sulphite content in crisp, fresh white and rosé wines; however you'll often find even higher sulphite content in a bag of salad from the supermarket.

TANNINS: These are naturally occurring compounds called polyphenols, which are found in many plants, most commonly in tea, but also in chocolate and wine, in particular reds. They give you the dry feeling in your mouth after you've swallowed the wine that makes you salivate. They dissipate when the food arrives and actually make everything taste a whole lot more delicious.

TERROIR: A magical French term which loosely translates as 'sense of place' – the geography, geology and climate in which the grapes for a wine were grown, and which can all impart unique characteristics on it in any given year. It gives the wine its unique identity card.

VIGNERON: A French wine grower. Often you'll have a wine farm (domaine or château in France) where the owner grows the wines *and* makes the wine. That's a vigneron.

VINTAGE: The year that the grapes for the wine were harvested.

YEAST: These do the hard work of turning sweet grape juice into wine . . . the sugar into alcohol. The type of yeast used can have a big effect on the flavour of the wine. Top wine growers will use naturally occurring yeasts, i.e. those that are naturally around in the vineyard, on the grapes and in the winery. These will start a fermentation and keep it going until the sugar is all eaten up. You can also buy commercial yeasts that are designed to do the job thoroughly and these are widespread.

Acknowledgements

I never thought there'd ever be a day where I'd be writing... 'Here is my book'. Of course, this delicious little volume wouldn't exist without a small army of magnificent humans who tolerated my chaos and championed my ideas but it definitely wouldn't exist without you.

So, my first and biggest thank you goes to you. Thank you for picking up this book, buying this book or giving this book. Thank you for the support you have given me, whether it's watching/sharing the wine clips on social media, messaging me for advice or recommendations or, of course, supporting this book. You've given me the ride of my life.

A heartfelt thank you, too, to Square Peg, the publishing team who commissioned this book and supported me in getting it done...

Marianne Tatepo, my team lead, you have been nothing short of outstanding. You somehow saw the glimmer of something worthwhile in my jumbled early drafts. You cajoled me when I got stuck and rallied me towards the deadlines with kindness and compassion.

Thank you to the two geniuses Marianne thrust upon me when I got bogged down in the weeds – Rachel Kenny, you were instrumental in getting order and structure to my garblings and Rosemary Davidson, you managed to flip a few words around in no small number of sentences to make even

ACKNOWLEDGEMENTS

me want to read them. In fact, my two weeks working with you, Rachel and Rosemary, were, oddly enough, some of my favourite moments of this entire adventure.

Big thanks go to Dominic Price, my agent, or I should say 'our agent' as it's Fred and me making this chaos together. Dom, you reached out to us at the very beginning and have held our hand through our entire journey thus far. Goodness knows the mess I'd be in without your guidance and support. You're a truly wonderful man and a great friend.

There are those of you who've inspired me and taught me from my early days in wine. My late, great Uncle Mick, Jack Scott, Gavin Quinney and John Worontschak. All of you have challenged me to look deeper into the glass.

Huge thanks go to my family. My two daughters Georgia and India and my two sons Fred and Billy, and my long-suffering best friend and wife of nearly thirty years, Beth. My poor children have had to learn quickly how to cope with their fifty-three-year-old dad ridiculing himself on social media while Beth, the rock of our family, has been keeping it all together. Without your support, particularly yours Beth, this book and everything behind it would have never happened. Thank you all, I love you with every fibre of my being.

My family beyond Beth and our four children get a bucketful of thanks too. My brother and sister, James and Charlotte, both cheering me on from the sidelines, and my incredible dad, Bill, who's now put down his chef whites and keeps us constantly entertained.

To my brother- and sister-in-law Tom and Emma and your families. Thank you for your incredible support, without which I think I'd still be scrubbing tanks at Thames Valley Vineyards.

ACKNOWLEDGEMENTS

And so to Fred, my eldest son, producer of all wine content that we send out and my business partner, this book would have never been commissioned without you. Thank you for all your ideas, your kindness, your unfailing support and your desire for adventure. I love the tussles and consider myself the luckiest dad in the world to be working with you.

This book is dedicated to my mum, Caroline Gilbey. Like the greatest of mums, you always told me I was much more than I ever believed. I hope you are seeing this now xx